COLLECTING
THE PAST

COLLECTING THE PAST

A Guide to Canadian Antiques

Ross Skoggard

OCTOPUS
PUBLISHING
GROUP

Canadian Cataloguing in Publication Data

Skoggard, Ross, 1949–
  Collecting the past

ISBN 0-409-90720-0

1. Antiques – Canada. I. Title.

NK1125.S56 1992   745.1′0971′075   C92-093105-7

Produced by B & E PUBLICATIONS INC.

Cover and Book Design by Design UYA Inc.
Typesetting by Attic Typesetting Inc.
Printed and Bound in Canada by Webcom

Distributed by
Butterworths
75 Clegg Road,
Markham, Ontario L6G 1A1

Published by
Octopus Publishing Group
75 Clegg Road
Markham, Ontario L6G 1A1

For my son

Contents

Introduction

ALTHOUGH some people had the foresight to begin collecting antiques in Canada prior to 1967, the antiques business received its most significant boost with Canada's centennial year. After 1967, the collecting of antiques became popular from coast to coast. As a result of this popularity several fine books were published by such authors as Donald Webster, Ruth and Blake McKendry, Howard Pain, Jean and Elizabeth Smith, David Newlands, Philip Shackleton, Gerald Stevens, Jeanne Minhinnick, Barbara and Henry Dobson, Catherine Thuro, Michael Bird, Una Abrahamson, Elizabeth Collard, Eric Arthur and Thomas Ritchie, and Hyla Waults-Fox.

Interest in antiques continued until the early '80s when the collectibles market merged with the now flourishing antiques business. Both areas of collecting soared to new price heights through the affluent '80s—buyers wanted the best and were willing to pay for it. However, as the best antiques became rare and priced beyond even what the most affluent could afford, collectors started looking around for new interests in antiques.

Although the market has been depressed through the current recession, a recurring growth is almost certain in the '90s. If you do not already have a collection, it's time to start one. Once you determine in which particular area you wish to become involved, start to learn all you can about your chosen field. Knowledge is the key to successful antiquing.

COLLECTING THE PAST is a good place to begin. This book is geared to the beginner to intermediate collector. One of the most difficult problems facing the antiques collector today is how to determine if a specific piece is a fake or spot a restoration. Ross Skoggard helps to address this problem in sections on different categories such as ceramics, wood, glass, paper, textiles, silver and plastic. The concept of whether or not an object has been misattributed or overly repaired, techniques of manufacture, finishes, methods of faking, correct cleaning and storage procedures for each of the above categories are all explored.

Another very important aspect of the book is the information on what makes certain objects more—or less—valuable than others, what makes one form better than another and how to attribute provenance.

Additional information at the back of the book includes a very comprehensive glossary of terms, a rough price guide, and a list of resources which includes names and addresses of large antiques fairs and flea markets.

The author's frankness yet emotional love of antiques is evident in the words in Chapter One—*"Antiques are documents of the past in addition to being mere decorations. They record information about the taste, cultural and domestic priorities, and the level of technical sophistication of the community that produced them. When a piece is thoughtlessly repaired or refashioned, that vital information becomes confused. As such, an antique that is an outright fake can be compared to a forged document."*

Bill Dobson
Publisher/Editor
The Upper Canadian

CHAPTER ONE

When Canadian Antiques Were New

THE vanguard of the semi-feudal society transplanted from France to the Bay of Fundy at the beginning of the 17th century arrived in small ships with little room for anything besides arms, tools and a few of the men's personal effects stored in chests.

It wasn't long, however, before craftsmen with the ability to fashion the superstructure of a European society from the raw materials of the Canadian wilderness arrived. These masons, smiths, carpenters, woodworkers and others were usually hired by seigneurs (land grant holders) for a minimum of three years. They were to provide homes and furnishings for the ruling class of churchmen and landowners in a style that would mimic as closely as possible what they left behind.

Thus in a few decades the seigneurs were able to obtain a few pieces of furniture made from local timber and other works of decorative art in the Louis XIII style.

These objects are at the apex of the Canadian antique furniture market. They are rare because after the Conquest, when many French aristocrats repatriated to France, they took with them much of what they had of value.

But a greater portion of this early Canadian heritage was destroyed in the devastating fires which ravaged the colony with depressing regularity. So chronic was the problem of fire in the towns of New France (where all the buildings were heated by wood throughout the long cold winters) that today there is only a solitary 18th-century building left in Quebec City. The rest—the churches, the schools, the mansions and their contents—have all been consumed.

Much of the remaining original furnishing in the habitant's cottages fell victim to changing tastes. Furnishings of earlier generations were generally held in low regard. Early pine armoires, tables and chairs, and

Detail of rococco carving on the door of an 18th-century French Canadian armoir.

Photo: The Royal Ontario Museum

the like, were considered *cochonneries*, a term used to refer to homely and embarrassing objects. They were too often gotten rid of as soon as a family could afford to order new furniture from a department store.

The disregard felt by the heirs of this early Canadiana is illustrated by the report from one prospective collector in the 1930s. Heartbroken to find a family taking a hatchet to one of the nicest armoires he'd ever seen, he asked why they were doing it. They replied "because old pine makes wonderful kindling."

So it's not just quality, but sheer scarcity that makes early French Canadian furniture and decorative arts among the most valuable Canadian antiques.

To help categorize what remains, it is useful to think of the colony of New France as essentially a *two-tier* society.

Settlement in the colony was encouraged by a system of land grants to court favorites. To make these lands profitable, seigneurs in turn encouraged the emigration of tenant farmers. The habitants, tenant farmers, wood cutters, fishermen and trappers who came over to occupy the second tier of Canadian society clearly had their own idea of what a home should be. They used their skills to reconstruct what they could of the peasant houses of their beloved Normandy and added their own interpretations of the finery glimpsed in the seigneurs' houses.

The craftsmen who made the furnishings for the two classes even had separate professional designations within the trade. The *menusiers* or joiners and woodworkers made the massive case pieces: the armoires and chests, the simpler tables and chairs. The *ébenistes* were the cabinetmakers who produced the more formal pieces for the manor houses and bishops' palaces: the chests of drawers with the *bombé* fronts, the delicately carved chairs, etc.

Two influences fed the remarkable flowering of the decorative arts in the colony of New France: the fur trade and an explosive growth in population. The rapid accumulation of wealth by the men who profited from the fur trade is evident in an 1805 auction notice in the *Montreal Gazette* for the sale of the contents of the house owned by the widow of fur baron Simon MacTavish, the head of the North West Company. It illustrates how very well some people lived in the colony:

"BY AUCTION
Will be sold...at the house of Mrs. M'TAVISH, going to England, all her most valuable furniture—consisting of FEATHER BEDS, Matresses, mahogany bed steads, chests of drawers, desks, a new piano forte, large dining tables, chairs, &c., sets of the most fashionable china, knives and forks in

cases, a quantity of silver mugs, spoons, forks, servers, &c.,
&c., sophas, sconces, looking glasses, carpets, old Madeira,
Claret, Port, Burgundy, and other wines of the first quality, in
bottles; an elegant new Phaeton, cabrioles, gig and chair,
several covered carioles, an excellent horse for a chair, &c.,
double and single stoves, with a great number of other articles.

ALEXANDER HENRY"

Quebec City was even richer. The lords of the colony entertained in a
style that was considered extravagant even by Paris standards. The
furniture of this particular period from Quebec City shows its distinct
French inspiration more effectively than the furniture made in Montreal.
It is more refined and better finished.

Then there was the second impetus: the explosive population
growth. From a total of 2,000 in the 1650s, the population grew to
82,000, in a little over three generations. Large families were encouraged by the church. After producing 25 children, the church policy was
to assume the expense for raising the 26th: a sort of raise 25, get one
free arrangement which evidently proved irresistible.

This burgeoning population inspired a frenzy of church building. A
seigneur was forbidden by law to construct a mill on his land—one of his
best sources of income—before he had built a church.

Of course, churches required decorating. Statues, altar pieces,
paintings and silver were necessary to complete even a relatively
humble church of the period. Yet the men who could produce this type
of skilled work were in painfully short supply.

To fill the need a crafts school, the first in North America, was
established in Quebec at the end of the 17th century by Bishop Laval
and the Intendant, Jean Talon.

Talon wrote "The young men devote themselves and attack their
studies in the classes for science, the arts, crafts and particularly
seamanship, with such enthusiasm that if their interest continues to
grow there is reason to hope that this country will become a training
ground for navigators, fishermen, sailors and craftsmen, all with a
natural disposition for these professions."

The Arts and Crafts School of the Quebec Seminary as it was
known, did not survive long; by the beginning of the 18th century it was
gone. But before its demise it had certified a group of master craftsmen
and laid the groundwork for an apprentice system that persisted in
French Canada for another hundred years.

Supplying the everyday needs of the ordinary householder were
independent craftsmen working out of small shops who would build the

Photo: The Royal Ontario Museum

The Church commissioned most early Canadian silver.

larger case pieces, like armoires, on a commission basis. Oral tradition reports that other woodworkers would travel the colony and board with a family while they made furniture, earning approximately 25 sous a day plus room and board. The craftsmen would saw planks as they were needed and meticulously fit and refit an armoire, say, fashioned of stiles and floating panels held together with mortise and tenon joints. These pieces ultimately resembled nothing so much as monumental architecture with scrollwork decoration and projecting cornices.

Typical of most émigré communities is an understandably nostalgic attachment to the styles currently popular in the homeland during the period they left.

In French Canada, for instance, Louis XIII forms lingered on, especially in the countryside, many years after they were no longer fashionable in France. Similarly, a century later, English-Canadian cabinetmakers continued to supply a demand for Chippendale designs some 20 years after they went out of style in England.

The conquest of New France by the British in 1760 further isolated the colony and arrested the stylistic evolution of its decorative arts. Most of the French aristocrats returned to France leaving a society where contact with the mother country was discouraged by its British conquerors who feared the ideals of the French Revolution would spread. Quebec remained fixed in a semi-feudal state.

In its early years English Canada (except for Newfoundland) was primarily a military base. Garrison towns from the maritimes to Upper Canada were supported by Britain, and the officers who ran them brought their own furnishings. When their tours ended and they returned home, so did their furniture. The first cabinetmaker in Halifax, Edward Draper, arrived in 1749 with the 2500 English settlers of the Governor Cornwallis expedition.

The civilian culture of English Canada received a major infusion in the early 1780s when the flood of Loyalists entered from the United States after the American Revolution. Soon to total 50,000, the influx of Loyalists of English, German, Dutch and Swiss background overwhelmingly preferred Nova Scotia as a destination. Among the nearly 30,000 who settled there were scores of cabinetmakers, carpenters, silversmiths and other craftsmen.

Working mainly in a Chippendale idiom from native pine, maple and birch, (although mahogany from the Caribbean became available when 4,000 feet were auctioned off in Halifax in 1786), maritime cabinetmakers left a body of work that, while a little more plain-spoken and subdued than its English and American models, is often pleasingly proportioned and well-made.

Diamond-point panels decorate this typical armoire.

Other Loyalists were directed to Upper Canada. Many came via a lake and river route through New York. The difficulty of the journey meant that they could bring very little furniture with them. Often they would order what they needed from drapers and cabinetmakers. Much furniture from old Upper Canadian homes was made in Albany, Rochester and to a lesser extent, Boston, New York and Philadelphia.

All Canadian furniture was essentially provincial in style compared to its English and American models, as evidenced by the simpler forms and techniques. Urban styles produced by trained cabinetmakers, or carpenter-made rural interpretations, often represent an apparent blending of influences. In fact much country furniture soon lost its distinctive national characteristics making it difficult to identify a piece as simply "Dutch," "English," or "German."

The trade in timber from Canada to Europe, and with the Caribbean, and the universal popularity of certain styles make it difficult to identify the origin of some early 19th-century furniture exclusively from forms or primary woods used. Experts, however, are able to make distinctions on the basis of secondary woods (i.e., woods that don't show) and hardware.

Three mahogany veneer Chippendale chests from 1790 made in the United States, England and Canada, may look superficially indistinguishable. But clues to identifying their countries of origin are there in the parts that aren't immediately visible. If the secondary wood is oak, for instance, the piece is almost certainly English. If it is pine and the hardware is English, the piece is probably Canadian. If the hardware is American and/or the secondary wood is a combination of pine and several others, you likely have an American piece of furniture.

The "Golden Age of Good Taste," as the 18th century is sometimes known, was over in Europe by the time the first settlers arrived on the north shore of Lake Ontario. The history of the decorative arts in Upper Canada therefore belongs essentially to the 19th century and reflects that era's obsession with reviving and combining a variety of earlier styles.

Among the most interesting pieces found in Ontario are in the Sheraton and Regency styles. Though long out of fashion in England, demand remained strong for many years for objects that reminded settlers of the homes they left behind.

English-Canadian cabinetmaking flourished between 1785 and 1820. There are no known pieces pre-dating 1785, and just 45 years later, the craft began to be overrun with factory-made pieces in the newly fashionable Empire style.

The result is that Empire, especially individually-made work c. 1820, is the last period to incorporate enough distinctive regional variations to permit it to be identified positively. With the volume of furniture coming out of the factories, many cabinetmakers became furniture retailers offering their own work alongside mass-produced items.

The third major European influence on the decorative arts of Canada is German. Arriving largely from Pennsylvania with the Loyalist wave of the 1780s and for 50 years after, German immigrants brought with them a penchant for large, simply-constructed case furniture often of pine and decorated with paint or imitation graining.

The families inter-married and soon the German influence became diffused throughout Upper Canada. Today much of what we consider painted country furniture made in Ontario can be traced to that early German influence.

The objects left behind by the pioneers and early families in this country are prized for their intrinsic charm, certainly, but also for the story they tell about the people who made them. In many cases a work of decorative art can tell you how its owner lived, how they adapted to the new country and even what they thought of themselves.

Antiques are documents of the past in addition to being mere decorations. They record information about the taste, cultural and domestic priorities, and the level of technical sophistication of the community that produced them. When a piece is thoughtlessly repaired or refashioned, that vital information becomes confused.

As such, an antique that is an outright fake can be compared to a forged document.

The fake object, whether it's a paper document or a work of decorative art, is accepted as genuine at a cost not only to its purchaser but to everyone interested in trying to gain insight into the past.

The damage done, for instance, by a forged will that perverts the intention of a donor towards his or her heirs will be obvious to everyone. What about a forged historical map such as the famous Vinland Map purporting to date from 1440 and offering proof that European exploration of the New World pre-dated Columbus? The discovery of this map, announced on the eve of Columbus Day in 1965 by Yale University, was one of the first salvos in the revisionist assessment of Columbus' significance that continues to this day. Traces of modern chemicals in the ink, grammatical errors in Latin and an uncannily accurate outline of Greenland have led scholars to doubt the Vinland Map's authenticity. Its historical significance may be minor: scholars know now that Columbus was not the first European to discover the New World, but countless other false documents have not left such a benign legacy.

Matters of history, dynasty and the like may hang on questions of a

Photo: Metro Toronto Reference Library

This Pennsylvania German chest is dated 1775.

paper document's authenticity. But the significance of other social issues also hangs on the authenticity of a painting or a piece of furniture or silver.

When a false object is accepted as an example of the work of a fine craftsman from a particular period, everyone's sense of quality is compromised.

A connoisseur's ability to "feel" that an object is "right" is based on considerable experience of comparable pieces from the same hand or the same period and region. When too many anomalous expressions have to be included in the canon of "right" pieces, the boundary between what is right and not right, authentic and inauthentic, becomes blurred.

Connoisseurship is the first defense against, but also the first casualty of, fakes and faking. When we are fooled, regrettably our appreciation for the quality of the best achievement in an art form is compromised.

And when we think less of the best that our artists can achieve, in some way it costs us all a little self-respect—as a nation, as a culture and as individuals.

CHAPTER TWO

Ceramics:
The Classic Collectible

CERAMICS is a field so vast that connoisseurs rarely know much about the subject beyond their own area of expertise. It has been said that in no other field are experts more dependent on makers' marks and, at the same time, more suspicious of them.

This is because ceramic objects are among the easiest to fake. The value of the raw materials in even the costliest porcelains is only a few cents. Molds can easily be taken from originals. The rest is simply paint.

In some cases signs of wear are one of the first clues to age. But since the forms and colors of valuable ceramics have been reproduced for centuries, wear alone will not distinguish between an original and an antique reproduction.

In some cases, lesser workmanship may be the giveaway, in such things as cruder colors or garish gilding. But for a beginner these clues are sometimes only apparent when compared with the original.

Porcelain is the aristocrat of ceramics. It is very strong and hard. While quite translucent, you can't scratch the body with a knife.

Invented in China over 1000 years ago, it mystified and obsessed Europeans almost as soon as it was imported. Great noblemen competed for prize pieces and all over Europe potters experimented to find the secret to true porcelain.

The closest they came to this was with a mixture of superior china clay and glass. It was translucent and almost white just like true porcelain, but not nearly as strong. This product, known as soft-paste porcelain, is very rare today and in some cases more expensive than real porcelain.

Porcelain was endowed in the 18th century with near magical properties. It was believed to ward off illness and to discolor in the

Photo: Metro Toronto Reference Library

Transferware was made specially in British factories for the Canadian market.

presence of poisoned food (in fact some of the alkali-based medieval poisons do stain porcelain.)

The discovery of the secret of porcelain was made by Johann F. Bottger, a self-styled alchemist who was imprisoned (after failing to make gold) by one of the most maniacal porcelain collectors of the period, Augustus the Strong of Saxony.

Augustus established a record price for porcelain when he traded a regiment of 600 cavalrymen for 48 pieces of Chinese porcelain.

Bottger convinced Augustus he could find the secret of porcelain and was released from prison to make the attempt.

In 1709 he succeeded, and a year later Augustus established The Royal Saxon Porcelain Manufactory at Meissen, Germany to produce it.

Silversmiths were retained to do the designing and the early production from the factory at Meissen was decorated much like silver holloware with techniques such as gadrooning, piercing, openwork, etc., borrowed from the smithing trade.

To protect what was virtually an 18th-century licence to print money, Augustus decreed that revealing the secret of porcelain's formula was punishable by death. But unhappy Bottger got drunk one day and told the formula to a Meissen factory painter who fled to Vienna with the secret to set up a rival factory.

Europe has a much older tradition of earthenware pottery. The body of this ware is opaque and bricklike and must be glazed: finished with a baked-on surface, if it was to be used for liquids.

From about the 18th century on, one of the cheapest and most common glazes found in European and North American stoneware is salt glaze. It is made by throwing salt into the kiln when the fire is at its hottest. The salt vaporizes and adheres to the red hot clay and then forms a grey-colored body which is sometimes decorated with a cobalt underglaze.

The most collectible North American specimens are those bearing a sort of calligraphic decoration showing birds, animals, flowers and the like, in cobalt glaze. Stamped with the name of the maker or the retailer who sold it, makes the piece even more prized.

The history of Canadian potteries, like the history of Canadian glass works, is one of a series of small to medium-sized potteries that struggled bravely to find a niche in the domestic market. But like the glass works, they were unable to compete ultimately with the flood of imported wares of all types arriving from Britain and later the United States. One problem was that Canada does not have much clay of high quality. In some parts there is enough common red clay for bricks and

Photo: Metro Toronto Reference Library

Salt-glazed stoneware is valued for its decoration and markings.

the most ordinary quality of crockery, but for anything better—whiteware and stoneware—the clay itself had to be imported.

In addition, Canadian taste was developed by imported wares with their printed underglazes and complex molding, features which technically limited domestic factories were unable to reproduce.

Early on there were remote rural markets that local producers supplied with utilitarian earthenware. But importers and their agents were aggressive marketers, and as soon as these outposts could be reached by bateau or cart, it seemed factory-made ceramics were being offered for sale.

And yet Canadian potters did succeed against the odds in at least starting up a number of factories. They sent samples off to the great international exhibitions of the day in Paris, Philadelphia and Antwerp, and they were noticed and commended.

Is it the slightly defensive tone of a Canadian manufacturer, or a clever merchandising tautology that comes through in promotional material from the mid-19th century that claims wares are "warranted equal to English of the same quality"?

A large percentage of the material the collector of Canadian ceramics has to work with was made abroad specifically for export to Canada. There are transfer-printed sets of earthenware with images drawn from recently-published engravings and lithographs.

Images from the War of 1812, Canadian and British genre scenes, politicians and advertising plates were imported in a variety of shapes, and from a number of manufacturers, giving an idea just how popular china tableware was in the new country.

On Dec. 9, 1844, one Halifax merchant advertised that he had received "300 Crates and Hhds (hogsheads) of China, Glass and Earthenware..." and was looking forward to more "expected per other... vessels to arrive."

The major share of the Canadian market for imported china was taken up by stoneware. Yet there continued to be a steady, if much smaller demand for porcelain.

Newspaper advertisements from the mid-19th century on seem to indicate that Worcester was a popular choice for Canadians, even if early announcements do not clarify in which Worcester factory the porcelain was made.

The ledgers of the Royal Porcelain Works in Worcester show that in mid-century the company was executing special orders for Canadian customers.

There were designs, colors and crests made-to-order for Alexander Levy, a Montreal china merchant, and in 1860 a quantity of wares was decorated with the Prince's three feathers and the maple leaf commemorating the visit to Canada of the heir to the British throne. These last were ordered in connection with dinners given throughout Upper and Lower Canada for the Prince and were afterwards auctioned as souvenirs.

At the other end of the ceramics spectrum were the crude earthenware jugs and crocks made from local clay by resident potters. If they were remotely located, these craftsmen may have enjoyed a monopoly for their immediate region. But as soon as transportation improved, importers made their products available and local producers were reduced to supplying just the bottom end of the market.

Not surprisingly, in the early guides for emigrants to Canada, opportunities for potters are hardly ever mentioned.

In 1832, writing under the pseudonym of "A Backwoodsman," Dr. William ("Tiger") Dunlop stressed that blacksmiths, tailors, tanners, shoemakers and others all had promising futures in the colony, but makes no mention of any need for potters.

Similarly, in VIEWS OF CANADA AND THE COLONISTS, by James Brown many trades were encouraged to emigrate to Canada in the 1840s, but potters were not among them.

The most successful and one of the most long-lived Canadian potteries of the 19th century was The St. Johns Stone Chinaware Company.

Founded in St. Johns, Quebec, in 1873 this well-capitalized concern attempted to compete head-to-head with the giant Staffordshire potteries in England in the production of whiteware. In the late 1870s, after a few shaky early years, the company began to actually make money. At that time it employed 120 workers, half French-Canadian and half Staffordshire English. The resulting line of china is very close to imported Staffordshire including one particular white wheat pattern and several tableware patterns that look identical to those imported from England. This ware generally can be identified as Canadian only by its mark.

By competing successfully for steamship and hotel accounts the firm was able to survive and even flourish. It was just after a new wing had been built, the workforce doubled and new equipment installed that a fire gutted the main building on March 4, 1893 causing $130,000 damage. The insurance covered less than half that and as a result the St. Johns Stone Chinaware Company closed its doors after 20 years of operation.

The balance of domestic production was lead and salt glazed earthenware. Some cobalt-decorated salt glaze crocks are now getting quite valuable. But like sgraffito and slip-decorated red earthenware

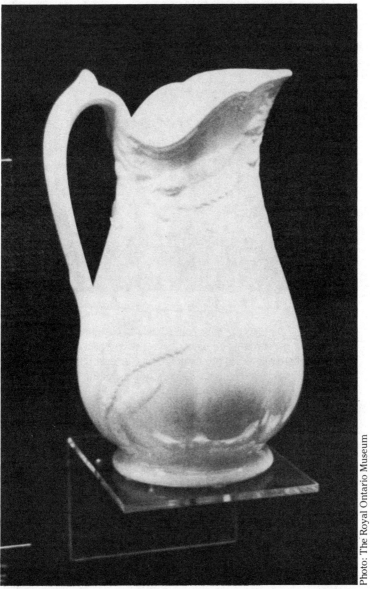

A white wheat-pattern pitcher from the St. Johns Stone Chinaware Co., 19th-century Canada's most enterprising pottery.

Photo: The Royal Ontario Museum

The mark of the St. Johns pottery.

from the 18th century, the most collectible U.S. earthenware, the means to manufacture reproduction pieces have always been widely available.

Since there are as yet no scientific tests for distinguishing between period and modern ceramics, successfully spotting fakes becomes almost a matter of individual taste.

Some experts warn collectors away from decorated earthenware that is "too cute," for instance. Because the value of decorated objects is a function almost entirely of "eye appeal," reproduction pieces are likely to look "overdecorated" compared to authentic examples. Once again it's a subjective judgment.

What to Look For

The value of finer china and porcelain can be diminished somewhat by repairs. Until recently most repairs were made with a paste that was different in composition from porcelain. It is opaque, doesn't ring when tapped with a coin, and shows up as a different color under black (ultraviolet) light. New compounds mimic porcelain much more effectively, are not distinguishable under black light, and top restorers say they are virtually undetectable.

Another cause for concern is the fact that many of the old firms are reissuing antique patterns made in the original molds. In a few decades these pieces will show the same wear marks that now make up the distinguishing features of the early product.

Care and Cleaning

The fragility of ceramics is part of their inherent charm and a contributing factor to their value. Pieces break frequently making perfect examples all the more rare.

In cleaning and storing ceramics you should always be careful you don't inadvertently damage the value of a piece by chipping, scraping or cracking it.

When you wash china use gentle soapsuds in a rubber tub or a basin lined with a towel. Wash one piece at a time and allow to air dry.

Earthenware stains may be removed with peroxide and gentle rubbing with a damp, salt-covered cloth.

Don't stack objects on a shelf without some sort of pad or newspaper to help prevent the unglazed foot of one piece scraping away the decoration on the piece beneath it.

Stains in the cracks of some pieces can be removed with damp salt or a solution of hydrogen peroxide.

Whether or not you have a piece to repair, a visit to a good restorer is very instructional. When you realize that even badly broken pieces can be made to appear perfect, you'll be much more careful when you buy.

Dealers can get good repairs done more cheaply than private individuals. Therefore, you are unlikely to recover the price of a good repair when you sell to a dealer.

CHAPTER THREE

Wood: Time Will Tell

AN organic material, wood never stops interacting with the atmosphere. It gives off water and gradually shrinks and grows lighter. It reacts with oxygen in the air and turns brown. It absorbs oil from its finishes and develops an unmistakable patina over the years.

A piece of wood is always ready to tell you its age; if you know how to ask it properly. And it answers most frankly in those unfinished parts that are exposed to air.

An understanding of wood begins with a knowledge of trees.

The world of wood is divided between hard and soft woods.

Soft wood, from a more primitive type of tree that is cone-bearing and (except for the larch) features evergreen needles, is soft because of its cellular structure. One type of cell performs both of wood's two functions: the conduction of nutrients from the roots to the leaves and back, and support.

Hard woods, from a more evolved, broad-leaved family of trees, has distinct cells for the two functions of conduction and support. The support cells are more densely packed. They are formed during the spring by the inner layer of bark, which creates the annual rings.

The proportion and configuration of support and conduction cells differs from species to species and accounts for the differences in wood's appearance and workability.

Tree species are distributed geographically in broad latitudinal bands. Near the equator are the vast hardwood forests from which come mahoganies, teak, afrormosia, rosewood and other exotics like tulip-wood and zebrawood.

More temperate zones yield hardwoods like oak, walnut, beech, chestnut, sycamore, ash, elm and birch. The softwoods, pine and fir, overlap these species and extend farther north.

Until the turn of the 16th century, nearly all wood workers were confined to working only with local species. Soon a growing scarcity of timber plus increased wealth and sophisticated tastes led to the importation of wood to Europe from abroad.

It's important to know what types of wood were available to cabinetmakers, and which ones were preferred for particular styles when determining whether a particular piece is genuine or not.

Mahogany was one of the first exotic woods imported to Europe from Cuba. The library in the Escorial Palace was furnished in mahogany for the King of Spain in 1584, the first use of the wood by European craftsmen.

Cuban, also called "Spanish" or "Santo Domingo" mahogany is extremely dense and strong. It is a deep reddish-brown color with a distinctive curl in the grain when specially sawn. Understandably it was the preferred wood by English cabinet makers from 1730 to 1800, and its strength and workability inspired, and perhaps made possible, some of the stylistic innovations of Thomas Chippendale and his contemporaries.

In North America mahogany never quite dominated the craft the way it did in England. Ample stocks of domestic maple, cherry and walnut meant New World cabinet makers often preferred those woods for making furniture in more or less traditional European styles.

Canadian parlor furniture from the first two quarters of the 19th century, was often made in figured (curly or tiger) maple, cherry or butternut (except in the Maritimes and cities on the St. Lawrence that could be reached by ocean-going ships). Built-in cabinets and rougher country pieces are usually found in pine which was invariably painted or finished to look like more expensive wood.

Pioneers were often obliged to make every sort of household utensil out of whatever material came to hand. In Canada, a country filled with vast forests, that material was wood.

In addition to spoons and bowls, mortars and pestles, everything from measures to candlesticks to neck yokes and butter paddles and even foot warmers was made from one of the native varieties of wood.

Burl grain and evidence of hand carving enhances the value of these small pieces of woodenware or "treen."

One specialty within the hobby is the collecting of maple sugar molds from Quebec.

There is no typical maple sugar mold. The molds for export sugar are very plain. They come in one, two and three pound sizes and usually consist of four side pieces and a bottom section.

For the domestic market, however, woodcarvers gave their ingenuity full reign. Fish, birds, houses and books were all carved into the

Photo: Metro Toronto Reference Library

A cabinetmaker's shop would have looked virtually the same from the 16th to the 20th century.

Photo: Metro Toronto Reference Library

Many early Canadian household implements were made of the material nearest at hand, wood. Above, a burl bowl.

multi-part molds giving collectors an ample and charming selection from which to choose.

The Centennial celebrations of 1967 inspired new interest in Canadiana. Canadian antiques began to be collected. Painted country pieces, with their cracked and grimy surfaces often held little appeal for the newly minted collectors of the '70s. Their solution was to strip the paint off and expose the attractive honey-colored wood underneath.

More sophisticated collectors realize that the surface of an old object is one of its chief glories. The form of an object was contributed by its maker, but the patina, the quality of its surface was made by its successive owners. It tells a story of how a piece was used and cared for, or neglected, and greatly contributes to its overall charm.

Today, original paint is much prized. Restorers take dozens of hours to carefully peel back successive layers of paint to the original surface. This, in part, accounts for its high price. You're paying for the object's antique value plus the restorer's time. High prices invite less scrupulous traders to "improve" a simple country piece with a nifty period paint job.

Almost invariably, however, there is some place, usually the back or bottom of a faked wooden antique that gives it away.

A whimsical Quebec maple sugar mold in the shape of a car.

The bottom of cabinet doors for instance will sometimes be over-looked by persons removing or adding paint from a piece. Here you may find drips of paint and stain from previous surfaces. A painted country piece with the original finish is rarer than one that has been restored to the original finish.

Things to Look For

When inspecting any piece of furniture pull it away from the wall and look at it first from a distance where you can get a sense of its proportions: you should see a pleasing ratio between the size of the piece and the scale of its parts. The most common means of "improving" furniture is to cut down large pieces into smaller ones that are more saleable. Experience in assessing pieces in public collections, good shops or auction previews will help you get a feel for correct proportions. For instance, tables with flaps or tilt tops should be examined with the flaps down because it's easier to assess the proportions this way.

The unfinished "private" part of a piece of furniture, its back and underside, give a franker account of its age and means of manufacture than its polished front. Pull out every drawer and see that they all exhibit the same style of dovetailing, same type of wood and degree of "air burn;" the brown, oxidized surface.

The panels of older case furniture will have been hand dressed. Shining a flashlight across the grain should illumine the tell-tale shallow grooves made by old hand planes with their slightly convex blades.

Since complete sets of chairs are always more valuable than the sum of the value of the individual pieces, its important to check each item to see that patterns of wear are the same on each one.

The most careful workmanship will not be able to make the newly-made sixth chair of an antique dining set, for instance show the same amount of shrinkage across one diameter of the turned elements, or weigh the same. Because wood constantly gives off water, older wood will nearly always be drier and lighter.

Moldings are delicate and will need replacing if they fall off. Look at these applied ornaments carefully.

Carvings will sometimes be added to plain pieces to enhance value. The knees on cabriole legs are a favored area for "improvement." The carving should "stand proud" of the leg, and be higher than the surrounding wood. If it is carved into the wood it is probably not original.

Check all moldings to see that they "agree": meaning they were made of the same material in the same way.

Check brasses with a magnet to make sure they are not electro-plated reproductions. Brass is non-magnetic; iron and steel are.

Lastly, there is nothing wrong with any kind of repair or restoration *as long as the dealer has made you aware of it and has reflected in the price the fact that it is not all original.*

Make sure you have the right to return the object within a reasonable time if you have second thoughts after getting it home.

All wood, when green, contains a lot of water. As it is seasoned, water evaporates from timber until it approaches atmospheric humidity. At this point the wood is stable. The cells won't shrink any further because no more water is leaving them. The wood can now be worked.

Since wood antiques were made, though, they are exposed to new conditions which can cause problems. Central heating has created a much dryer environment and wooden objects are once again loosing water.

Wood radially shrinks across the grain as it dries, and joins made from once stable wood can become loose as the parts shrink to new dimensions.

The metal parts used in and on wood furniture are another feature experts like to check carefully. The methods used to make nails have

Photo: The Royal Ontario Museum

Signs of wear like those near the top of the door are typical in painted antique furniture.

obviously evolved in the past 170 years. Handwrought iron nails with pyramid-shaped heads are supposed to be a warrant of antique authenticity for a piece dating pre-1830, as are blunt end, hand-cut screws. They are good indications, but remember that old nails can be driven into new wood, just as new nails can be found in old wood. Further evidence that an old nail or screw is indeed original is sign of corrosion in the nail or screw holes themselves.

Brass fittings are often replaced. Original brasses on an old piece are a genuine rarity. Look at the backs of drawer fronts for signs of plugs, or bolt holes.

Stripping was a fad in the '70s that was very convenient for furniture fakers of the time. One of the hardest problems for the craftsman who was engaged in making a saleable piece from two or more period fragments, was getting the finishes to agree. Two pieces 150 years old hardly ever show the same patina. Unless the finish of one or both was altered, the "marriage" would be obvious even to the most gullible collector. The solution was to dump everything into the strip tank, and this is one reason why original finish is so highly prized among knowledgeable collectors.

Care and Cleaning

No piece of antique furniture can withstand the unnatural dryness of centrally heated houses in winter without proper care. Polishing with a good wax polish is necessary to seal the pores of the wood in order to keep as much of its natural moisture in as possible. Cracking and splitting will result if you neglect to polish.

Humidifiers, single room or central, are a help, and even vases or bowls of flowers help keep the air from becoming too dry.

Be careful to keep fine pieces out of the direct sunlight. Their surface will bleach and the glues—particularly under walnut veneer—can pucker and crack as they dehydrate.

Use cotton rags and apply polish sparingly. Work it into the wood with a circular motion. Buff it after it has had a chance to sink in. Solid woods can withstand hard rubbing, but not delicate veneers. Waxing should be done about every six months.

Before polishing brass handles and escutcheons apply a protective coat of paste wax on the area around the brass. Metal polishes can discolor wood.

Once they are completely dry, water rings can sometimes be removed with turpentine. Let the turpentine soak in and leave it overnight, then polish.

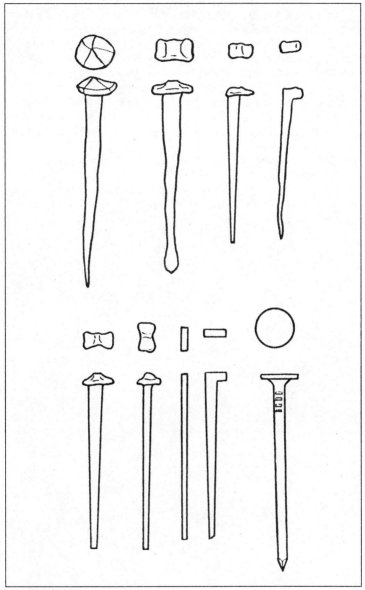

The evolution of nails.

Alcohol marks can be treated in much the same way. If they have actually damaged the surface of the finish (varnish can be soluble in alcohol,) rub very lightly with glass paper, the finest grade of sandpaper, then polish with a brown shoe polish in a color closest to the wood's. If this fails then expert refinishing may be necessary to restore the surface.

Ink stains dealt with at once can be minimized. Take up as much of the ink as possible with blotting paper, sponge immediately with fresh (unpasteurized) milk if its available, and clean with water. Use unsalted butter in place of unpasteurized milk if you don't live near a dairy farm or a health-food store.

Grease marks and stains can be removed with blotting paper under a cool iron.

Wilted flower petals can be a problem as they can leave water stains. And pollen contains a natural dye which will mark wood. Use the ink treatment for these stains.

CHAPTER FOUR

Glass:
A Material That Doesn't
Show Its Age

GLASS goes back. It's older than European civilization. Heating sand and alkali in a furnace until it melts, forming it and letting it cool until it hardens has been the basic technique for producing some of the most universal household implements for centuries.

From the collecting point of view, the very timelessness of the formula is one of the problems. The material is very inert: it doesn't dry out like wood does, doesn't develop a patina, making it very coy about its age.

The difference between free blown pieces made in Canada's first glass factory at Mallorytown, Ontario, in 1840, for instance, and modern Mexican reproductions may not be scientifically demonstrable.

Glass is the most easily and most often faked collectible. The *faux* piece only has to achieve a plausible form. Age and wear impact very little on even very old glass, so there's no real basis for judgment other than rightness of form and decoration.

From long experience with authentic examples in any art or antiques field, connoisseurs build up a sort of mental data bank on what objects from a certain period should look and feel like. Scrutinizing an object provides reassurance of a piece's authenticity or evidence of its invalidity. Then it is a matter of checking and inspecting particular details to confirm or disprove the original hunch.

Glass can be very challenging because the material itself doesn't "age" like wood or silver. The proven techniques of manufacture of even the oldest examples are still practised today by master craftsmen. So the expert generally stays with the original hunch. There is very little

A sugar bowl from the Mallorytown Glass works, c. 1839.

Photo: The Royal Ontario Museum

in the way of a "cross examination" that can be conducted on a piece of antique glass.

Interested Canadian glass hobbyists soon learn the story of the rise and fall of numerous little factories across the country beginning with the Mallorytown factory in 1839.

Window glass and bottles were the standard product line of these early plants. Typically, 20–25 blowers would be supported by the same number of assistants, packers, sales and administrative staff. The completion of the rail connections in 1856 meant bigger markets could be served, and plants expanded.

But it also made the Canadian market—3,700,000 strong in 1870—attractive to the much larger and more efficient U.S. and British glass firms.

A 15% import tariff—eventually raised to 17.5% in 1874—was finally imposed to try to save the Canadian manufacturers.

This compares to the minimum 30% import duty the U.S. levied on imported glass from Canada.

In 1871 Canada imported $581,966 worth of glass products, and manufactured only $292,130 worth.

When Sir John A. MacDonald was re-elected in 1878 with a promise to raise the protective tariff for Canadian industry, several new glass factories were set up to compete for the newly protected market.

Some made holloware, some window glass, but all faced the common problem of producing for a widely dispersed home market of 3,700,000 in competition with U.S. and British manufacturers who were producing as well for their own much larger markets.

Gerald Stevens, a pioneer and scholar of Canadian glass divided his subject into three neat categories. He termed pre-1900 Canadian glass Early Canadian Glass. It was manufactured before 1900 by 19th century techniques and was either free blown or mold blown.

Canadian Glass from 1900–1917 was made using the same techniques.

Twentieth-century glass made in Canada is distinguished by the fact that it was made using more modern mass-production techniques. Many examples are nevertheless rare because patterns become obsolete.

Free blown is the technique of shaping the molten glass or "metal" at the end of a hollow tube using gravity and the maker's breath, which can inflate the blob of glass like a balloon. It is a skilled job and every piece of free blown glass is one of a kind. The works at that first Canadian glass factory in Mallorytown, Ontario were free blown.

Mold blowing is a slightly less skilled job. The metal at the end of the rod is blown into a mold which provides a uniform shape to each piece made within it.

Molded pieces include those made with a mold and a plunger to force the glass against the mold.

There is only a handful of authenticated specimens from the Mallorytown Glass Works. All show a pontil mark, a scar where the blow pipe was broken off the finished piece. The appearance of this mark on the pieces indicates that the Works did not even have a grinder to remove the mark. These Works stayed in operation only about 15 months or until 1840.

Succeeding companies include the Hamilton Glass Works, 1865–1895; and the Burlington Glass Works, 1875–1909. The latter was the most prolific Canadian factory of its day and contributed more than its share towards the value of all the glass manufactured in Canada.

THE YEAR BOOK AND ALMANAC OF CANADA 1876, enumerates the size of the industry for that year. In all there were six companies listed, employing 309 males and no females. Wages paid for the year were $104,800 and the value of raw materials consumed was $102,275.

The precarious state of the industry is indicated in the last set of

DOMINION GLASS COMPANY LIMITED

Head Office   ·   MONTREAL

FACTORIES AT

MONTREAL, TORONTO, HAMILTON, WALLACEBURG, REDCLIFF

C—"B" COLLAR   B—"A" COLLAR   A—"A" COLLAR

No. 106 ONE PIECE LAMP

Photo: From *Canadian Glass, 1825–1925* by Gerald Stevens

Page from the Diamond Glass Co. catalogue of 1902.

figures: the value of articles produced (but not necessarily sold) — $293,130.

By looking at price lists for the year we can deduce that the total production of Canadian glass factories for the year amounted to more than 1,000,000 pieces.

During American Prohibition, Canadian distillers were allowed to export a substantial portion of their product to the U.S. for "medicinal purposes." Some of this product naturally went astray and earned the reputation in the speakeasies and flapper parties of the U.S. as being of very good quality indeed. Illegal bootleggers and distillers in the U.S. tried to take advantage of the good reputation of Canadian booze by counterfeiting the labels as well as the bottles and flasks used to ship it. In an effort to foil these practices, Canadian glass houses were asked to change the shapes of Canadian bottles. But almost as soon as a new bottle design appeared, it was copied and so had to be changed again. This continued until repeal, leaving a fascinating sideline for today's hobbyist.

Free blown paperweights were never made in quantity in Canada. But practically everywhere else in the world, buyers were found for these small jewel-like pieces of ornamental glass. They have been eagerly collected for a long time and the price of glass paper weights has been spiralling upward for more than 50 years. In that time many hundreds of reproduction weights have come on the market. Carl Dreppard, author of the FIRST READER FOR ANTIQUE COLLECTORS tells of the artful stratagem employed by a little old lady collector in New York in the 1940s. She would enter a shop and announce "I collect fake or newly made paperweights. Do you have any? Don't hesitate to unload them on me. That's what I collect. I can't afford the old ones."

With this approach she has bought not a single fake. But she has culled from the "wrong" ones offered her quite a few that she believed were real — and at a bargain.

Canadian Factories

Other early factories, their dates of operation and best known product known to glass collectors, include:

—The Napanee Glass House, Napanee, Ontario; 1881–83. The Napanee house made a free blown, German-style mercury-silvered candlestick in its short years of operation.

—The Toronto Glass Company, Toronto, Ontario, 1894–1900; known for whimseys; mold made, sandblasted paperweights and glass drapes, a popular window dressing at the time, made from chains of colored glass loops.

—The Sydenham (Dominion) Glass Company Limited, Wallaceburg, Ontario, 1894– made molded glass tableware and free blown whimseys.

—The Ottawa Glass Works, Como, Quebec, 1847. Produced inexpensive bottles.

—The Canada Glass Works Company Limited, Hudson, Quebec, c. 1871 made bottles, telegraph insulators etc., as well as a very popular small hand lamp.

—John C. Spence, Montreal, Quebec. 1854–1867. Spence was the first documented glass stainer in Canada.

—Foster Bros. Glass Works, St. Johns, Quebec, 1855–1880, made many types of containers, and telegraph insulators.

—St. Lawrence Glass Co., Montreal, Quebec, 1867–1875, made a wide selection of tableware and lamps.

—The Excelsior Glass Co., St. Johns, Quebec, 1879–1880, and Montreal 1881–1885, is a parent firm of the Dominion Glass Works. It was supposed to have produced two special collector's items: the Beaver Goblet made of flint glass in a three-part mold and decorated with six beavers and three maple leaves and inscribed "St. Jean Baptiste, Quebec, 24 Juin 1880." The other is a plain goblet commemorating

the first Ottawa Exhibition and is embossed "Exhibition 1878.
A.R.D." But now the source of these two especially collectible goblets is
in doubt.
—The North American Glass Co., Montreal, Quebec, the successor to
the Excelsior Glass Company.
—The Diamond Glass Co. Montreal, Quebec, 1892–1903.
—The Diamond Flint Glass Company, Montreal 1904–1913, succeeded
the above firm and made a quantity of tableware and insulators.
—The Nova Scotia Glass Company, Trenton, Nova Scotia, 1881–92. The
earliest documented glass works in the province, its prospectus printed
in the Eastern Chronicle of New Glasgow affirms the intention of the
company to make "tumblers, goblets, all kinds of glassware for general
use." It was absorbed by the Diamond Flint Glass Works for a payment
of $2,000 in 1892.
—The Humphrey Glass Works, Trenton, Nova Scotia, 1890–1914, Moncton, New Brunswick, 1915–1920, made items in the pattern known as
the "tassel and crest."
—The Lamont Glass Company, Trenton, Nova Scotia, 1890–1902, was
absorbed by Dominion as well. In their 12 years of operation they made
an assortment of tableware decorated with sandblasted designs.

Care and Cleaning

Glass should never be kept near a sunny window. Some formulas of 19th
century glass are apt to change color in ultraviolet light. Also the glass
can act as a lens and focus hot spots on walls, floors and furniture
causing scorch marks and even starting fires.

Iridescence is a type of finish on glass that can turn a common form
into a rarity. Be aware, however, that the process is no longer a secret
and iridescence can be applied to pieces by anyone with access to a few
common chemicals and a kiln.

Check pieces for evidence that the rim has been ground down to
remove a chip.

Old, authentic paperweights of good quality were usually well cared
for. Fakes are sometimes "aged" with scratches.

CHAPTER FIVE

Paper:
Worth More Than the
Paper It's Printed On?

MORE than any other category, the value of a paper collectible is determined by factors extraneous to the labor and the skill involved in its manufacture. One sheet of paper is very much like any other. What makes one a museum piece and another fit only for fish-wrapping is the status one has over the other as an historical source.

Pieces of paper really are the bane and the glory of any society. On them are written sonnets and solicitations, invitations and advertising messages and everything in between.

Paper ephemera collecting is a specialist's hobby, and like most collecting hobbies, it turns its practitioners into part-time historians.

A kind of paradigm of collectibles generally, in the sense that every object of age is a kind of document of the society that produced it, the importance of authenticity in paper documents is perhaps more readily appreciated for the novice. What, after all, is the value of a forged will or map? Authenticity in antiques is important not only because it affects overall value for an owner, but because we understand and appreciate the past in part through it's decorative arts legacy.

A piece of paper is transformed by what's written or printed on it from a sheet of bleached plant fibers to an historical token.

The card made to commemorate the rookie season of a great professional ball player, the first edition of a work of classic literature, a firsthand account of an important political event transform paper into coveted relics of past deeds.

At the top of the Canadian hobby are books recounting the discovery of the country. Yet many of the most valuable books of

Paper collecting opens avenues into all aspects of the past.

Canadiana were neither printed nor written in Canada. The first printed reference to Canada in English is from THE NEW FOUNDE WORLDE, OR ANTARCTIKE, WHEREIN IS CONTAINED WONDERFUL AND STRANGE THINGS, AS WELL OF HUMAINE CREATURES, AS BEASTES, FISHES, FOULES, AND SERPENTS TREES PLANTS, MINES OF GOLDE AND SILVER, not quite a literary fraud, but a literary sleight-of-hand published in London in 1568. The first-person account by a Franciscan friar is based on conversations with Cartier, but was passed off as his own experience.

Since books about Canada were more popular in the 17th century than actually visiting the place, several travel books of the era are similarly semi-fictional. This doesn't stop them from being highly collectible. Like fakes generally, they present a stereotype of their society's expectations for a certain type of object from a particular era.

Non-literary works are sometimes more relevant to historians. Researchers find that merchandise catalogues, bills, brochures, and posters are often more revealing than hours spent studying secondary sources.

Browsers of second-hand book stores will confirm that the flavor of life from the 1950s or '60s is often more vividly brought to life by a specific magazine or a directory than a dry, sociological dissection.

Some collectors look for examples of the first books printed in Canada. These are almanacs. And the first book bearing an illustration printed in Canada is THE NOVA SCOTIA CALENDAR FOR 1776.

Other types of sought-after Canadian "firsts" include first native language prayer books and first town directories.

The first printing press in Western Canada was a converted fur press. The type was made with lead from the lining on tea chests. Ink was a rudimentary mixture of lampblack and oil.

On this makeshift machine, in a Methodist mission 300 miles north of Winnipeg, a Cree hymnal, the first book published in western Canada was produced by Reverend James Evans in 1841.

The first half-tone reproductions of photographs in the world were published in Montreal for the *Canadian Illustrated News* using a process invented by James Augustus Leggo in 1869. They appeared there until 1872 when Leggo moved to New York to establish the world's first pictorial newspaper, *The Daily Graphic*.

Early advertising materials are collected also, but all early paper material became scarcer still in this century.

Paper drives during the two world wars may have salvaged millions of pounds of paper, but they also contributed to the complete destruction of countless irreplaceable documents.

Other printed matter was less likely to be considered waste paper.

Pulp paperbacks are collected for their lurid cover illustrations.

The development of lithography meant decorative pictures were now within the reach of the masses.

Catalogues are of interest in and of themselves, but they are also attractive to a wide range of non-paper collectors. For instance, the catalogues of glass factories are invaluable in identifying where which particular patterns were made and when.

As you develop a collection in any field, you will want to keep an eye open for documentation in the form of catalogues or advertisements that may help to positively identify your objects. This kind of documentation adds to the historical interest and therefore the value of a collectible.

Relatively new to the field of paper collecting are paperback book and magazine collecting.

Made for the mass market and hence, comparatively inexpensive, paperback books and magazines were made to be read and thrown away. The ones that have survived intact and in good shape with retrospective interest: articles on movie stars who died young, like James Dean and Marilyn Monroe, for instance, or books by mystery and science fiction writers who later may have developed cult followings are being collected. These can sometimes be picked up at yard sales for

From California come indications that literature about the counter-culture is becoming collectible.

Photo: Popular Culture

pennies, yet are worth over $100 in some cases to specialist collectors.

Cover art is one prominent collectible feature of pre-1960 paper-backs. Graphically illustrated to catch the eye of a browser with the promise of a good juicy read, many covers from the '50s are kitsch masterpieces.

Drug literature collecting is a hobby that is starting to come into its own in, naturally enough, that cradle of collecting hobbies, California. Apparently the actress Winona Ryder's father has a booming mail order business out of Berkeley selling books, pamphlets, posters etc. all having to do with recreational drug use.

One of the cheapest collecting hobbies to pursue is matchbook cover collecting. Begun around the turn of the century as the brainchild of a brewery salesman, the printing of advertisements on matchbooks produced billions and billions of examples until the decline in the popularity of smoking and increased printing costs made the medium cost ineffective.

Interestingly, of these the most collectible are covers with the striker printed on the front of the book. These all bear the legend "Close Cover Before Striking." After somebody had the brilliant idea of printing the striker on the back of the cover, to make the book a little harder to accidentally set afire, this legend was dropped.

At club meets covers are auctioned off for pennies apiece. They are simply marvelous works of graphic art, evoking the glamour of a movie star, the sophistication of a restaurant or the splendor of a natural attraction, all on a surface no bigger than a couple of square inches.

Stamp collecting is obviously a classic field that is very well established. Some of the most valuable Canadian stamps were printed on laid* paper. The 12d black from 1868 showing Queen Victoria as a young woman facing out (not in profile) and the 3d beaver printed in red are two prime examples that were printed on this unusual stock.

Subsequent stamps were printed on wove paper and glued and perforated. Any stamp with a young regal Victoria facing out and denominated in pence is clearly a rarity.

Strangely one of the most interesting Canadian stamps is one that was never issued. Just before Canada changed its currency to the current dollar system and each province was still printing its own stamps, the postmaster general of New Brunswick, Charles Connell ordered a series of stamps from the American Bank Note Company in the new denominations. The sets of 1c, 2c, 5c, 10c, 12½ c, and 17c stamps arrived at Fredericton in sheets of one hundred. Examining officials were a little alarmed to see the 5c stamp. Instead of Queen Victoria, the stamp bore a likeness of Charles Connell.

The impudent Connell was asked to resign, whereupon he bought up the entire run of half a million stamps, burning all but a few.

Photography is a field that has been growing fast in popularity for 20 years and is an even more recent field of paper collecting that brings a more direct description of its period.

Some of the earliest material for collectors of Canadiana was shot by itinerant photographers who toured the country in the mid-19th century taking portrait daguerreotypes. These are collected both as much for the molded plastic, velvet-lined case as for the image.

Later on, traveling photographers would make postcards of towns, villages, natural monuments and even disasters. These were printed up in editions of several dozen and then sold to a local shopkeeper. The enterprising nature of these early postcard makers is evident in an example owned by a Toronto collector. It is of a spectacular train wreck in northern Ontario. The date of the wreck is printed on the card, and the card itself is postmarked just one day later.

---

* Laid paper is distinguished from wove paper by a grid pattern left on the paper from the screen with which the pulp is pulled from the water.

Fine prints: etchings, lithographs, engravings, etc. have always been produced to be collected.

In the Canadian fine print field, artistic quality takes a back seat to historical interest. Much of the image making being done in Canada up until this century was in the nature of topological sketching. Views of specific terrain designed for military planning purposes, often by army officers, these landscape images were meant to supplement the information on maps.

One of the most important Canadian prints is also one of the homeliest. A wood engraving of the Habitation at Port Royal is a small out-of-perspective image of the first settlement in Canada. It was published in Samuel de Champlain's VOYAGES...ET DECOUVERTES...1615–1618 in Paris in 1619.

In this print a group of buildings form a quadrangle in a field still littered by tree stumps. It is interesting to note that the image contains a vertical view of the planting scheme for the courtyard. It is laid out in the style of a formal French garden, testimony to the determination of even the very first settlers to import a European way of life to the wilderness of the new world.

Things to Look For

When buying an old print, map or document, use a magnifying glass and examine it out of the frame and in good daylight.

You'll be looking for watermarks: identifying crests or words in the body of the paper itself, also for any tears or repairs. Remember, these are all more visible when the sheet is backlit.

If the print was made by an *intaglio* process (etching, aquatint, mezzotint, etc.), check to see that the image goes right to edge of the platemark: the indentation made by the metal plate on the damp paper when it went through the press. Some prints may be mere photocopies that have approximate platemarks impressed after the fact.

Sports cards are a prime example of how collecting can become a huge money-making operation. More money is spent annually on cards than on actual tickets to major league games in the U.S. And where there's money, there's sure to be fakes.

Because sports cards are not fine prints to begin with, good color photocopies on the appropriate stock have fooled even experienced collectors.

Never buy an expensive card in its plastic holder. Take it out and examine it next to a "common" card from the same series to make sure the stock is identical. One card expert claims he can tell a genuine card by simply smelling it. Sometimes the smell from the flavorings in the gum originally packed with some cards may linger.

Care and Cleaning

It's important to handle old prints and documents as little as possible. Try to avoid picking a work up by the tips of your fingers, the weight of the paper alone might be enough to cause a tear.

Make sure there are no metal clips or staples attached to any piece of paper you are putting in storage. Atmospheric moisture will eventually cause the metal to corrode and leave permanent rust spots.

Always use archival quality (acid free) boxes and folders for storing prints and other paper objects. And keep paper things out of the attic or basement where fluctuations of heat and humidity can occur.

Also important are the use of archival quality mats and backing when framing things.

Strong light is very damaging to paper as well. Don't hang prints and papers where direct sunlight can shine on them. The light will cause the pigments in the ink and paint to fade and also attack the paper itself. If you can't avoid strong light in a room, at least frame the piece with ultraviolet-resistant plexiglas instead of glass.

Books

Always remove a book from a shelf to dust it, and when you do remove it, don't pull it from the top of the spine where it may be weak. Push the books on either side back so you can grasp the entire spine. Keep the book closed so dust doesn't get caught in the pages.

If you pack books too tightly on the shelf you can also do damage to their bindings.

Storing newpaper clippings or pressing flowers within the pages of a book can harm the paper of a book.

"Mint" in book dealers' parlance is a very specific and strict category. To qualify as mint, a book will have:

1. original covers intact
2. undamaged dust jacket
3. no library markings
4. original, unbacked spine
5. hinges and joints uncracked or repaired
6. no foxing (tiny rust marks) staining, brown, yellow or moldy pages
7. uncut; with fore edges untrimmed
8. plates intact

9. all pages present including fly, printed pages, errata slip (if any) and plates
10. the "point," particular characteristic or flaw that identifies the edition

Humidity and temperature extremes can harm paper too. Dampness encourages mildew, while dryness will make the pages brittle. The ideal humidity is between 55 and 65%, with the ideal temperature between 60 to 70 degrees Fahrenheit.

CHAPTER SIX

Silver:
The Metal and Its Marks

LUSTROUS, soft, "good-natured" when alloyed with a small amount of copper, silver is rare enough to be coveted, but, unlike gold, not so rare that it can be afforded only by kings and plutocrats. Every developed nation has its silversmiths but English silver is the most sought after around the world because the flowering of English silversmithing occurred in an environment of strict government regulation of silver content.

Mandated by law in 1290 to a proportion of 92.5 parts silver to 7.5 parts copper, objects made from British sterling silver were tested at one of several assay offices in the British Isles. If it passed it would be stamped with a mark known as a "leopard's head."

The original system used to gauge the purity of gold and silver at the assay offices was an extraordinary combination of science and art. Needles produced from various alloys of the metal, including the correct one for sterling silver, were streaked across a touchstone of flinty black slate called basanite. The marks were moistened with saliva or an acid which would dissolve the metal's impurities. The streaks of the control needles would be compared with ones left by the objects being tested.

This test was more accurate for gold than silver and in the beginning of the 14th century another method was devised called "assay by the cupel." For this test 10 or 20 grains of metal were scraped off an object, folded in a thin sheet of lead and heated until it glowed red. The impurities would form an alloy with the lead leaving a tiny button of pure silver. This would be weighed giving a much more scientific indication of the sample's purity. If, in the Guild of Goldsmith's amalgam of Old English, French and Medieval Latin it was found "alloy de bon esterlin," the piece received the "touche" or stamp of the assay office. If it was below standard, the entire piece was crushed and returned to its maker.

Photo: The Royal Ontario Museum

English silver is prized the world over for its purity and excellent design.

Clearly the assay stamp was a very valuable attribute for a silver object to have. Silver tableware, etc. might be privately commissioned, but could not be sold on the open market without it. Laws were intentionally strict to prevent fraud, but in 1720, as taxes of sixpence per ounce began to be imposed on silver articles (which had to be paid in advance before a duty stamp with a likeness of the reigning monarch would be applied), so did efforts to circumvent the assay office.

The most popular dodge was to bring small finished pieces in for assay, receive the marks, then cut them out and incorporate them into much larger, heavier pieces. To prevent this in 1739 the assay office declared all makers' marks obsolete and registered new ones. This didn't work either, so they took to stamping assayed pieces with the marks as far apart as possible in an effort to make them difficult, if not impossible, to cut out and reuse.

The discovery of "let in" marks, ones identifying the piece as the work of a famous maker from an earlier reign, is still one of the most common indications of fake silver.

The "leopard's head" sterling mark never originally represented a leopard's head at all. The confusion about the lion figure used in the sterling stamp arises from the use of heraldic terms by the Guild of Goldsmiths in which "leo" means lion and "leo partant" meant a lion "regarding as he passes," a device from Henry II's coat of arms. Thus the King's mark was known as a "leo part" mark, which was basically heraldic shorthand for a lion "partant." The "leo" of the sterling mark was still recognizable as a lion through the centuries, perhaps less shaggy but still wearing a crown, until 1820 when he succumbed to his nickname and became a leopard.

The place to begin when contemplating the purchase of English silver is with a thorough investigation of the marks. The history of the Guild of Goldsmith's struggle with the assay office has meant sudden changes in the correct form and style of silver marks so it is wise to ask to see a copy of a definitive book of marks like Sir Charles J. Jackson's ENGLISH GOLDSMITHS AND THEIR MARKS which every serious silver dealer should have on hand.

Things to Look For

Check for corresponding marks on cover and body of two-part pieces: tankards, tureens, entrée dishes, coffee, tea and chocolate pots, ewers, etc. Variations in the marks could indicate a "marriage" of fragments from objects of different years or makers, lowering the overall value. Beware of worn marks in places where a piece is unlikely to have received much wear, like the base of a coffee pot. This could indicate "let in" marks.

Original armorials. When wealth began to be accumulated by a rising middle class after the Industrial Revolution, many *nouveau riche* industrialists applied their own arms to silver plate acquired from older families. Again, a specialized book will indicate the appropriate engraving style for various periods. Look also for indications that armorials have been erased: suspiciously thin body in the center of platters, on the lid and body of holloware.

Later decoration. With all the good intentions in the world, the Victorians thought they were genuinely improving earlier silver by adding chased (a feature added to the outside with hammer and punches) and engraved decoration to its otherwise plain surfaces.

Electroplating. Careless repair or ordinary metal fatigue can cause hairline cracks in the body of old silver. The only way to repair and render usable holloware meant to hold liquids that has been damaged this way is to have it electroplated. The color of the silver will be harsher and have less sheen owing to the fact the new surface is comprised of pure silver, lacking the "bloom" of sterling with its copper alloy.

Electrotyped reproductions. Complete sets of a dozen pieces of tableware are worth more than the sum of the individual items, so there is real incentive for unscrupulous individuals to "fill out" a set with reproductions. Electrotyping is a process for casting silver from a mold. Again, the giveaways are the hallmarks. They will appear gritty in the reproduction piece and in exactly the same position as one of the originals. Reproduction candlesticks are manufactured in the same way.

Canadian Silver

Because of its Loyalist history, there is a fairly good selection of English silver in Canada, especially in Ontario. The family silver would have been one of the items brought over from the old country by emigrating families. It was always readily convertible into cash and more than any other heirloom, accrued sentimental associations.

The highest prices paid for Canadian silver are for pieces made in Quebec in the 17th century. There is a quantity of ecclesiastical silver made expressly for church and cathedral altars, in addition to domestic silver made for the aristocratic French families. These are sometimes identified by makers marks, but as there were no assay laws in the New World, the other marks can be confusing.

A considerable part of the overall output of early Canadian silversmiths consisted of trade silver, so called because it was carried all over

Rare early Canadian ecclesiastical silver is sometimes "created" out of more common American examples by altering the marks.

the continent by fur brigades to trade with the natives. It is found in the form of crosses, gorgets, brooches and other ornaments.

Trade silver, being generally crudely fashioned from thin coin silver, has been faked for years. Be very wary of unmarked pieces in forms not found in public collections. The amount of fake trade silver available vastly outnumber pieces of the genuine article.

Marks in general are a problem in assessing North American silver. English or American pieces, especially ecclesiastical silver, have been stamped with Canadian marks in order to be passed off as the rarer Canadian variety. All over North America, silver made by makers of English background was stamped with devices to mimic British marks. These are very idiosyncratic. The definitive book on the subject is John E. Langdon's CANADIAN SILVERSMITHS: 1700–1900.

The larger market in Canada was always for items made in base metals: pewter, brass and iron. The forms in pewter whether made in Canada or elsewhere, reproduce those made in silver and are now more common. At auction an écuelle, or covered, two-handled porringer of silver, sells for over 20 times the price of the same form in pewter.

Things to Look For

Canadian silver has been seriously collected only for the past 50 years or so. As in all collecting, the successful hobbyist will focus a particular interest as much as possible and buy the best he or she can afford. Canadian spoons made by the firms that were eventually absorbed by Henry Birks and Sons can be collected for under $100 a piece, and sometimes are still found at flea markets and yard sales. Relevant firms are Ellis, Roden and Ryrie. Presentation silver is another underdeveloped field. Trophies and loving cups, given as awards or to commemorate an event—especially if they have some historical association—are likely to go up in value. Look also for early 20th-century pieces made by Petersen and others in a style reminiscent of Georg Jensen, which will follow the upward price trend for work by the Danish silversmith.

Care and Cleaning

Be careful when you clean silver. You can harm its value when you use patent cleaning agents. Many commercial silver cleaners have abrasive powders suspended in a liquid which takes off a fine layer of the surface as it cleans. One of the glories of antique silver is in its patina, its silken, mellow surface acquired after generations of handling and diligent,

These 19th-century Canadian spoons were made on King St. in Toronto.

gentle polishing. Over-rubbing with an abrasive cleaner can harm the patina and therefore the beauty and value of an old piece.

Paul de Lamerie, the great 18th-century Huguenot silversmith prescribes the use of "warm water, soap and sponge and a dry soft linen cloth" to clean silver.

Keep silver dry as moisture will cause it to tarnish. To store, wrap in black tissue paper to keep out light which also accelerates tarnishing. White tissue paper is a second choice. Avoid newsprint as the chemicals from the ink can react negatively with the silver.

If a piece is so tarnished that it is actually stained, de Lamarie advises rubbing the piece using a damp cloth and going with the grain; that is from top to bottom for straight-sided pieces and with a circular motion for "salvers, ewers and basins."

Keep a chamois leather cloth especially for cleaning silver and nothing else, and if you must use chemical cleaners do so very, very sparingly.

One old-fashioned remedy endorsed long ago by Paul de Lamerie to clean badly tarnished silver involves skim milk. Soak a badly tarnished piece briefly in skim milk. Let the milk dry on the surface without rinsing. When it is completely dry rub with a soft cotton or linen rag and finish with the chamois.

Now that conservationists understand restoration and repair processes on the microscopic level, we can see that this method also has its drawbacks. The lactic acid in milk that chemically removes tarnish can eventually leave microscopic pits as it eats silver, its copper amalgam, and solder, at different rates, leaving a piece more prone to tarnish because of its greater surface exposed to air.

Another old remedy that worked when the oldtimers discovered it but may not work now, is the recommendation for storing silver with moth balls. The idea is that the camphor in the moth balls displaces oxygen which tarnishes silver. The problem is that modern moth balls contain much besides camphor, some of which may in fact speed up the discoloration of silver.

You should be very sparing with a patent preparation cleaning fused plate (Sheffield or electroplated pieces) because by wearing away the silver surface you are gradually exposing the copper beneath.

A fine watercolor brush that is frequently washed is recommended for dusting.

Selling Silver

The minimum value of any piece of silver is its melt price or value as

Photo: Chadwick & Shand

Reminiscent of the work of Georg Jensen, this covered bowl was hand made in Canada by Petersen.

bullion. Silver prices fluctuate daily but you can use this equation to arrive at a fair price: obtain the rate times the Troy weight, number of ounces the object weighs, less the proportion of copper in the alloy and the weight of the solder used to fashion the piece.

Most pieces are worth more than the melt price, especially if they are correctly marked.

CHAPTER SEVEN

Textiles: Women's Sanctioned Art Form

NEEDLEWORK has always been a sanctioned arena for women's artistic impulses. When oil painting, acting, and writing were still not considered quite respectable enough for genteel young ladies, crewel, needlepoint, lace making, etc. were nevertheless smiled upon.

She could do it right there in the parlor, a model of industry and thrift. In some traditional cultures, like among the Indians of Bolivia, a young unmarried woman wore a sample of her weaving from her belt as a kind of advertisement of her value as a wife.

Textiles, therefore, are some of the most complete, sometimes the only, evidence of the often thwarted artistic output of this entire sex.

That needlework such as samplers was considered an appropriate and eloquent medium for womens' non-verbal expression is borne out by several literary references. In ARCADIA, Sidney wrote: "And then, O Love, why dost thou in thy beautiful sampler set such a work for my desire to take out?"

Shakespeare made two allusions to samplers. In TITUS ANDRONI-CUS he makes Marcus recall to his niece Lavinia how Philomela, deprived of her tongue by Tereus, "In a tedious sampler sew'd her mind."

Helena pleads to Hermia in A MIDSUMMER NIGHT'S DREAM to recall how they once had "with our needles created both one flower,/ Both on one sampler seated on one cushion . . ."

Contemporary scholars are beginning to recognize antique and vintage needlework as the vehicle for a sublimated feminine artistic impulse and look to it for more complex expression than it has been credited for up to now.

Samplers sewn on linen cloth reached their height of popularity in the 18th century. They were typically a young girl's introduction to needlework.

Over time samplers became much more than just stitched "exercise books." Although there were standard stitches and forms a girl was supposed to demonstrate, there was considerable latitude for imagination. She would work favorite quotations, scenes and animals into her sampler.

Often touchingly personal, these samplers are among the most prized today, especially if they are signed and dated.

Unfortunately the act of framing samplers has exposed them to danger from the acids contained in the backboard and mats used.

Silk work is embroidery usually made by older women using stitches and motifs perfected since their sampler-making days. These works are often based on paintings and engravings. Stitched representation of a loved one's tomb, etc. (called mourning pictures) are frequently worked in silk.

Crewelwork is embroidery with wool on a linen background. The name derives from "crewel" a word for a worsted yarn that has been twisted.

It is most appropriate for large pieces such as counterpanes, but seat covers, pictures, petticoat borders and pockets were also done in crewelwork.

White work is a name for white embroidery on white fabric. It is often seen on christening gowns, handkerchiefs and very delicate bodices.

Beadwork is needlework incorporating beads. In the 18th and 19th centuries bead-embroidered pieces of canvas were made into slippers, ornate pictures, sewing and desk accessories and small bags for women called reticules.

Needlepoint is the covering of a cloth backing with stitches of colored yarn or thread. The tent stitch was used in Berlin work* during the Victorian era when complicated pictures would be reproduced with dozens of colors from a sort of paint-by-numbers drawing.

Quilts are among the most popular needlework collectibles. They display very well on the wall and are still widely available and relatively inexpensive.

Quilt making is a nearly universal craft for making warm and decorative bed-covering out of scrap material.

---

* Berlin work is an ambitious form of needlework intended to make pictures rather than just two-dimensional designs.

Martha Scratch Mifflin made this quilt in 1870 from the uniform her husband wore in the Fenian Raids.

*A 19th-century crazy quilt made from scraps of salvaged material is
embroidered with dozens of images from women's lives.*

Dating is difficult without a knowledge of imported cottons. A general guide is the fineness of the sewing. But modern craftspeople can sew just as fine a stitch as anyone's great-grandmother, if they really want to.

Many Canadian handmade textiles and rugs were made in workshops that were established to bring a source of income to communities dependant on seasonal employment. The model for these enterprises is very old.

In 1705, the ladies of Quebec were awaiting the ship *La Seine* with its cargo of cloth and dresses when news came that it was captured by the British. Mme Lagardeur de Repentigny persuaded local farmers to raise flax and sheep and their wives to spin and weave it into material. She started workshops where linen, serge, etc. were made, greatly improving the social life of the colony as well as its economy.

Grace Helen Mount of New Brunswick similarly inspired a cottage industry in New Brunswick which evolved into the Charlotte County Cottage Crafts at St. Andrews.

Further east, hooked rug making was established by the Canadian Handicraft Guild to bring off-season employment to communities like Cheticamp in Cape Breton, Nova Scotia.

Similar rugs made at the Grenfell Mission in Newfoundland are collected all over North America.

Things to Look For

Earliest quilts were made from scraps of imported fabrics: chintzes, and other plain and printed fabrics. The shortage of fabric that was endemic to most rural areas necessitated this form of recycling. Some old quilts can show up to 4,000 pieces of material.

The earliest North American quilt designs are bilaterally symmetrical. Later designs from the middle of the 19th century feature all-over pieced-block designs.

Dyes are another indicator of age. Look for greens that have faded to blue or yellow, a stable green dye was not available until fairly recently.

There are some 3,000 known patchwork quilt patterns. Sophisticated collectors search out the less common designs in strong colors and in good condition.

Crib quilts like any small-size antiques have an appeal all their own and sell at a premium. Be careful that the one you are considering buying hasn't been cut down from a full-size quilt.

Smell Testing Fabrics

Sometimes the only way to identify a fabric is to burn a few threads. Use an odorless flame like a candle. Take a few threads and move them closer to the flame. At a certain point the thread will burn. Clues to the fabric's make-up will be in the smell, appearance of the residue and whether the thread ignites. This chart is from THE TEXTILE COLLECTORS GUIDE by Elyse Sommer.

fiber	odor	residue	flammability
cotton	—	—	will support a
linen	burning paper	gray soft ash	flame: no ash
rayon	—	black bead	burns
acetate	vinegar	dark bead, hard	will flame,
triacetate	—	—	some melting
wool	singed hair	crumbling dark ash	doesn't melt
silk	—	—	—
chinon	—	—	—
nylon	celery-like	hard tan bead	will melt
qiana	sweet	hard tan bead	melts
polyester	sweet, floral	hard tan bead	melts
acrylic	sharp, chemical	black bead	burns
modacrylic	sharp chemical	hard black bead	does not burn

Care and Cleaning

Textiles should be handled with extreme care.

There are special soaps and cleansers for textiles. Pure soap flakes are the best and most commonly available cleanser. Remember, soap flakes must be dissolved in hot water, but allow the water to cool before immersing any vintage textiles.

When wet, all fabrics are much heavier. Be careful not to tear them when lifting them out of the basin. Don't scrub; let the soap do the work. Simply swish the fabric around gently in the water. Don't wring, place in a towel and roll. The fabric should always be supported as it air-dries. Never machine-wash or machine-dry fine fabrics.

Protect your fabrics with acid-free tissue paper or old sheets. Don't store in plastic as moisture can become trapped inside and start to mildew.

CHAPTER EIGHT

Plastic: The Quintessential 20th-Century Material

PLASTIC is the "first magical substance that consents to be prosaic," wrote the French philologist Roland Barthes. Whatever he meant by that statement, there is no disputing the fact that plastic is defiantly unnatural, and when you learn to appreciate that, you're on your way to falling in love with this quintessential 20th-century material.

"Plastic" derives from the Greek "plastikos" which means moldable. As such, the first plastic is really quite ancient. Lacquer was developed from tree resin by the Chinese in 1000 BC and made into all sorts of decorative objects. The first modern plastics were likewise derived from natural sources.

Papier maché made from paper and glue was molded in the 19th century into furniture, tea trays, work and writing boxes, etc.

Bois Durci produced in France between 1855 and 1890 was made from powdered wood and blood or egg albumen. It was molded into cameos and used to decorate furniture.

Gutta Percha derived from a southeast Asian bark and, 100 years ago, was made into everything from furniture to jewelry to picture frames and match boxes. It disintegrates easily so early pieces are very rare. Today it is still used as the cover for golf balls.

The first semi-synthetic plastic was *vulcanite*, a form of natural rubber hardened with sulfur and developed by Charles Goodyear in 1838. It is still used for pipe stems, and was commonly seen in fountain pens, telephones and imitation jet jewelry.

Celluloid was patented by the Hyatt brothers in the U.S. in 1869. It is considered by collectors to be one of the most beautiful plastics. It could be stained beautifully to imitate tortoise-shell, pink coral or pearls.

Photo: The Royal Ontario Museum

The fact that celluloid was highly flammable did not stop this versatile plastic from being made into elaborate hair combs in the 1920s.

Imitation tortoise-shell combs made from celluloid were an essential part of the well-dressed woman's coiffure in the early years of this century. She might have worn up to a quarter pound of the material in her hair for a complicated "do," a frightening thought when you realize the material is highly flammable.

But it was in this century that the material really came into its own. It is ideal for mass production. It need only be colored as a raw material, molded, and it's finished. It needs no varnish or paint, and can be made into virtually any shape at all.

The streamline shapes of the 1930s and '40s that have been seducing collectors for years now, may owe more to the perogatives of compression molding plastic and metal than any designer's freewheeling inspiration.

To get a material in and out of a one-piece mold it is necessary that the form express a continuously larger circumference from a point at the center of the mold to its edge. Any "bombé" shape that bulges out and then contracts, cannot be made in a one-piece mold. Streamlined "bullet" shapes, on the other hand, are perfect.

Is it just serendipity that a fashion for these shapes arrived just as

Collectors all over the world appreciate Addison radios made in Canada in the 1930s for their colorful Catalin boxes.

mass-production techniques for plastic consumer items were being perfected? Or did the compression molding machinery draw the profile for consumer products of the decade, with public taste obliging manufacturers after the fact?

The futuristic shapes of radios and other consumer appliances have been avidly collected ever since we stopped visualizing the future as a space-age fantasy. Now, especially since fashion has been in a retro mood for years, these jaunty space-ship seltzer bottles and Mix Masters™ look terribly naive and quaint.

The very material of plastic contains some of this naive optimism. As petro-chemical amalgams were made into icons of the "good life" for upwardly mobile suburbanites, some contradictions of the culture seem to be built into the material of plastic itself. Today we realize some plastics emit nitric gas, others leach sulfur, still others are dangerous environmental pollutants, yet within the memory of many people these new seemingly innocuous substances were welcomed as mediums of ease and convenience. And they were fashioned into the mass-consumable and disposable artifacts to which the culture has become self-destructively addicted.

Depending on age, the two indicators of value in plastic collectibles, are either the form or the material. *Parkesine*, considered the first plastic made, was manufactured in England from 1855 to 1868 and was molded into common objects like book covers, shoe horns, fishing reels and door handles.

Its inventor Alexander Parkes is considered a kind of prophet of the modern consumer world because in a paper delivered to the Royal Society of Arts in 1865 he described his search for a material capable of replacing all previously-known natural plastic substances such as ivory, tortoise-shell, horn, etc. The replacement of those materials became, of course, one of the first applications of modern plastics.

Today, anything made of Parkesine is a museum piece.

The form of a piece of early plastic is often of secondary concern, unless you are dealing with tableware where some of the larger pieces are quite rare.

Radios and handbags were two consumer products that exploited the potential of plastic for whimsical form and color, and both are well-developed collecting fields. Minor variations of a certain radio, for example, the Toronto-made Addison from the 1930s, make a big difference in price. A particularly striking or unusual color combination, or a phenolic (Bakelite) rather than Catalin body will command a premium in the market.

Handbags were usually made out of heat-formed sheet acrylic. They were a fad that started with the carriage trade and the first models were quite expensive. You could get one in the early 1950s at Saks Fifth Avenue in New York City for $50. In a very few years, however, the product was knocked off in little factories all over the U.S. and the price, as well as the cachet, of acrylic handbags began to decline.

But like the radios, they display wonderfully. In their own way they bespeak the giddy optimism of the middle years of this century.

Many contemporary objects of plastic are collected by far-sighted investors. However, here form is of the utmost importance, unlike early plastic collecting. Industrial designers, Ettore Sotsass Jr., Mario Bellini, George Sowden, and Dieter Rams, to name a few, are considered the modern masters of product design. Their designs in any material are collected.

Care and Cleaning

Though they don't rust or tarnish, plastics do age and deteriorate in their own unique way. Light will fade Ebonite™ and Bakelite™. Celluloid will melt in its own nitric fumes if it's not kept well ventilated.

To care for celluloid that has begun to go soft, some experts recommend that you soak it in a solution of washing soda for two or more weeks, dry thoroughly for several days and coat with a layer of nail varnish, which is usually made from cellulose nitrate or cellulose acetate. The varnish helps to form a barrier against oxygen.

Others warn against using anything that can interfere with the free circulation of air around a piece, necessary to carry away the corrosive fumes. Since some plastics can release oxygen, varnishing can actually lock in the problem making it worse. It is therefore necessary to make a positive identification of the material you're working with before you try any restoration at home.

To clean most plastics simple soap and water is fine. But don't soak early plastics, like casein, in water.

CHAPTER NINE

Selling Your Antiques: How to Get the Best Price

WHEN you first attempt to sell something from your collection at a good price, it won't take you long to realize that you are swimming against a strong current. The whole antiques market is geared to buy low and sell high. Private collectors are supposed to oblige by selling low and buying high. To do otherwise requires a considerable amount of organization, energy and knowledge.

There's a good reason why vendors of dry goods and groceries are called "merchants," and sellers of antiques, coins, art and other collectibles are called "dealers." It has to do with the fact that unlike dry goods, there is no set price for antiques, just an agreed price between a willing buyer and a willing seller.

The whole key to receiving a fair price for your items is finding a willing buyer and not being an over-willing seller.

Nobody wants to appear too suspicious, but not to be a little suspect is to be completely crazy. Whenever you dispose of your collectibles you are in danger of being taken advantage of. Don't sell if you are in desperate need of money. It's far better to pawn your treasures than to sell in haste and for too little.

An example of a successfully postponed sale involved the painting by Rembrandt, *Aristotle Contemplating the Bust of Homer.* Alfred Erikson, an American advertising man, bought the masterpiece from the New York art dealer Duveen in 1928 for $750,000. When the stock market collapsed a year later Erikson needed money. He convinced Duveen to "hold" it for him until he could buy it back. Duveen gave him $500,000 and in 1936 Erikson was able to redeem his painting for $590,000.

His good sense paid off. He was able to enjoy his investment for the

Photo: The Royal Ontario Museum

Where you sell and how you present your heirloom platter can have an effect on its price.

rest of his life and in 1962 his widow sold the painting to the Metropolitan Museum of Art for a record sum of $2,300,000.

Successful private selling is best done by advance planning. The more time you have to sell, the better the price you're likely to get.

A person reaching the age of 60, for instance, might start to think about what kind of home he or she will require after they retire. If it's to be a smaller one requiring fewer furnishings, they should begin at least to think about which objects they would be willing to sell and how.

Resist the urge to just chuck it all except for a few mementoes when the time comes. Check price guides for the value of everything. You may be astonished to learn the value of the toys and dolls the kids outgrew 30 years ago.

Older pieces could prove a puzzle. About three-quarters of the letters I get from readers of my column "The Collector" in the *Toronto Star* can be summarized as "what is it?" and "how much is it worth?".

Before you can learn how much it's worth you have to know what it is. Start by noting down everything you can tell about an object from observation: what it's made from, what it might have been used for, how long you've had it, where you got it, how big it is and so on. Take a stab at what country it comes from, if it isn't marked, and what period, too.

With a hypothesis you have something to prove or disprove as you research your object.

Many museums in Canada still hold identification clinics, where one day each week a curator will spend an afternoon with the public helping to identify their objects. Auction houses are other valuable sources of advice. Some dealers are generous with their time and expertise, but if you plan to sell to one, be aware that you're putting him or her in a conflict of interest situation. If they assess your treasure too highly you won't be ready to entertain their low offer. In any case, before the object has been positively identified, it's still too early to set a price.

When you know what you have and have found out something about its value from price indexes or auction catalogues, it's time to find a buyer.

There are pros and cons for each of the main outlets available to you.

Dealers

If you want to learn about how to spot repairs, reproductions and fakes, watch an experienced dealer go over an object he or she is considering buying. Be prepared to have everything wrong with the piece spelled out for you.

The reasons offered why a dealer may not want to pay your price are many. Typically your object is "not the right color...too small...too large...out of fashion...funny signature...poor condition...repaired...". You should beware of a situation where your object is disparaged in this way, yet the dealer still wants to make an offer. You are being softened up, made ready to accept a price lower than the one you want. Get a second opinion.

When offering group of items or the contents of a house, be careful when an experienced buyer wants just a portion: you could get "picked," have the most valuable items taken and be left with the dross.

Techniques to fool the unwary include the request to the seller to identify the most valuable item in the group after an asking price has been established. The buyer is relying on the seller to make a mistake by choosing something with sentimental but no real collectible value. The buyer may then offer a lower price for the rest, including the few real treasures.

Alternatively, a dealer may lavish praise on some insignificant items, say they are "too rich for my blood," and offer a small sum for the remaining pieces: the ones he or she *really* wants.

One man's junk is another man's museum piece. Make yourself knowledgeable about what you plan to buy or sell. This chair is rare because such objects were replaced by pioneer families as soon as they could afford something nicer.

Photo: From Collection of the Author

Handmade dovetail.

Your goal when selling to a dealer is to find one who already stocks items similar to yours. That indicates he or she has clients in your price range. If you sell good pieces to a dealer of inferior merchandise he will turn around and sell them to the more appropriate dealer. He can only make money by offering you a price below wholesale.

Selling on consignment condemns your object to second-class status in a shop. Since he or she has no money invested, the dealer will always tend to steer interest away from your pieces toward the ones he or she owns. But if you do consign, get a detailed document listing the description, the cost price to the dealer, a commitment as to who is responsible for breakage or loss, and a set deadline for the consignment after which the piece will be returned to the consignor.

Private Sale

Since in most cases you can expect little more than the wholesale price when you sell to a dealer, many sellers will try to reach the retail buyer directly. Again there are advantages and disadvantages.

The first place to look for a buyer is among your family or friends. Perhaps your piece has been admired for years by people who have

Photo: Metro Toronto Reference Library

Nineteenth-century factories like this one could undersell individual craftsmen.

seen it in your home. Let your circle of friends and acquaintances know you are selling and tell them to spread the word. If a friend is interested in buying let him or her know how you identified the piece and how you established its price, indicate price guides or auction records for the latter. Be straightforward. Say how much you could expect from a dealer or at auction (less commission) and ask a slightly lower price which includes a personal discount. A sale made this way is saving you time, trouble, and the expense of searching farther afield for a buyer.

It's important to get paid right away or make detailed arrangements for payment. That way you can sell a collectible and keep a friend, too.

Flea Markets

If you have a number of pieces to sell consider renting a booth for a weekend at a popular flea market. Outdoor booths or tables in summer can be had for $25 and up. Price your things plainly, but be prepared to give a small discount to satisfy a hesitant buyer and close a deal.

Decorators and Interior Designers

Decorators and interior designers are potential customers for art and fine home furnishings. They are entitled to discounts from showrooms and dealers, but if your things are well-priced you could find ready buyers. List your objects for sale and send it to decorators' offices or advertise them in trade journals. Decorators will sometimes act as agents for preferred customers, selling your things on commission to their own clients.

Collectors

Collectors are often the most motivated buyers. If they need one or two pieces to complete a set, and you have them, you could get a good price. The only drawback is that such a collector can be a very shrewd bargainer and is highly unlikely to tell you that he or she has been searching for years for just what you are offering. In these transactions proof of ownership, provenance, authenticity and value will help you get your price.

Institutions

Sometimes you can get the best "price" by donating your object to a charitable institution. Your piece will be appraised and you will get a tax receipt for its market value.

Charity Sales

Charity thrift shops and sales can also offer tax receipts. Since charities can be in competition with each other, you can sometimes negotiate a very favorable assessment of your treasure between two or more registered charities.

Auctions

On the plus side, a good auction is supposed to attract a roomful of buyers ready to compete for the better things offered. Try to get your consignment into a catalogue sale which will attract the interest of buyers from far afield who may place bids even if they don't attend a sale in person. The risk of selling at a loss on the night of a snowstorm to a half-filled room of bidders can be hedged if you negotiate with the auctioneer a reserve price below which you will not sell.

The process is initiated with an appointment either at the firm's offices if the objects for sale are portable, or at the seller's house if they are large. The auctioneer, or his or her representatives, will then give an opinion as to how much an object is likely to fetch. If the estimate sounds attractive, then work out the details. Make sure you have a clear understanding of what the reserve price will be, if any, and what the auctioneer's commission will be. Will you pay a commission on the gross realized by the entire consignment or on individual lots? What is the insurance cost, who pays it? Who pays delivery charges and what are they? When will the sale take place? Will there be a catalogue? Will your things be illustrated? If so, who pays for the photograph? How much? What is the size of the mailing list? Should any item be cleaned or repaired, what is the charge? What other goods or collections will be offered with yours?

It is in the auctioneer's best interest to hold a successful sale with your consignment. Make sure you have a clear understanding of the division of responsibility for the sale to avoid any unpleasant surprises later.

Although not considered to be a problem in Canada, auction prices can be artificially manipulated in the sale room.

Practices that inflate prices include the trick of taking bids "off the chandelier."

This is where the auctioneer will repeatedly raise the bid by pretending to acknowledge the instructions of a bidder located at the back of the room, apparently, (or hanging from the ceiling) when there is really only one person still bidding.

Working against the seller to keep prices artificially low is the nefarious "ring." This is a group of dealers or collectors who have decided in advance not to bid against one another but rather to bid as a syndicate for a few desirable lots.

After the things they want have been knocked down at a discount (often the most desirable pieces in a sale,) the dealers hold a private auction among themselves. The difference between the hammer price and the private price is split amongst the group.

The loser is the consignor whose property is sold at prices that don't always reflect its true value.

Selling Deportment

How you look and how you behave in front of a prospective buyer can affect the price you'll get.

Some tips:

1. *Telephone or write for an appointment. Some dealers won't buy from unknown individuals off the street. Give your bona fides.*
2. *Dress well. A subtly negative tone may emanate from dealers approached by poor or shabbily dressed persons offering merchandise for sale. Look as if you might be a valued customer in the future and you'll get more consideration.*
3. *Try to get the dealer to make the first offer. Some won't, insisting that you make the first move so they can counter with a lower offer. If you have to make the first offer, state a price higher than the one you'll accept.*
4. *Be assured. State your price firmly and confidently, not apologetically. Hesitation indicates you are unsure of yourself and perhaps the value of the piece.*
5. *Drop names, especially if they're true. An association with a well-known collection or an historical personage makes any antique easier to sell.*
6. *Time your approach. Dealers buy before shows and exhibitions.*

Appendices

Pricing

Compared to prices listed in guides, certain standard repairs should be worth a more or less standardized discount.

Repairs will influence price depending on the age and availability of an object. Certain pieces that have been repaired are so hard to come by that collectors will pay almost full price for them.

Here is a guideline for more common items with well-done invisible repair work.

Furniture

Repair	Discount
Good to excellent chests of drawers, pre-1867	
replaced brasses	10%
refinished	10%
one front foot replaced	10%
two rear feet replaced	15%
four feet replaced	70%
Good chair, pre-1867	
slip seat replaced	0%
block braces replaced	0%
one or two leg brackets replaced	0%
all leg brackets replaced	10%
one leg replaced	33%
top crest rail replaced	15%
Early 19th-century veneered furniture	
one drawer re-veneered	50%
total re-veneer	90%
Good table, pre-1867	
top replaced	50%
one plain leg replaced	20%
four carved feet replaced	90%
Desk, pre-1900	
missing interior compartments or drawers	30%
Plated silver	
needing replating	50%
replated	5%
foot or handle replaced	75%

Glossary: Plastic

ABS—A Terpolymer made from acrylonitrile, butadiene and styrene which is chemical and impact resistant and suitable for furniture, computer housings, etc.

Acrylic—A hard thermoplastic best known as a glass substitute under trade names Perspex, Lucite and Plexiglas.

Amino plastics—Made from ammonia-based compounds urea formaldehyde and melamine formaldehyde.

Aniline brown—Dye originally produced from indigo which turns brown on exposure to air. Now chemically produced, was used to paint tortoise-shell markings on sheet cellulose.

Bakelite—Trade name for phenol formaldehyde (Phenolic) produced by Bakelite Corp.

Blow molding—Inexpensive way to form thermo plastics in hollow molds.

Casting—Way of forming resin poured in a mold and hardened.

Cellophane—Dupont trade name for sheet cellulose.

Celluloid—Flammable thermoplastic made from cellulose treated with nitric and sulphuric acids. Trade name for cellulose nitrate.

Cellulose—Fibrous matter in plant cells.

Cellulose acetate—Molded to form eyeglass frames and toothbrushes and as transparent packaging film.

Cold molded plastics—Plastics pressure molded at room temperature and cured by heat.

Compression molded—Common method for shaping thermo-plastics like Bakelite. Material is compressed against a female mold under heat and pressure.

Elastomer—Synthetic rubber.

Ester—Compound produced from an acid and an alcohol.

Extrusion—Method of shaping by forcing softened material through a die.

Filler—Additive to polymer to improve its properties, commonly wood pulp, cotton flock or talc.

Flash—Line of excess plastic along mold joins, usually filed off the finished piece.

Flow lines—Pattern made by plastic filling a form, can be used decoratively.

GRP—Glass Reinforced Plastic: a type of fiberglass with polyester resin.

Hard Rubber—Rubber vulcanized until extremely hard.

HIPS—High Impact Polystyrene.

Injection Molding—Mass production technique where plastic granules are heated and forced into a mold.

Melamine—Melamine formaldehyde, a tough, glossy plastic usually strengthened with wood pulp.

Monomer—Simple plastic usually mixed with others to form higher density polymers.

Mottle—Incompletely blended colored molding powders.

Nylon—One of a group of tough thermoplastic polymides.

Organic compounds—Compounds containing carbon molecules.

Parting Lines—Line on a molded article left by parts of the mold.

Phenolic—Phenolic formaldehyde best known under the trade name Bakelite.

Plasticizer—Additive to make a plastic more flexible.

Polycarbonate—A tough thermoplastic substitute for glass.

Polyesters—Compound esters.

Polyethelene—The most common plastic in the world, can be flexible or rigid.

Polymer—Another word for plastic that is made from one or more monomers.

Polymerization—Chemical process of linking monomers to make polymers.

Polypropylene—A thermoplastic polymerized from propene, harder and more rigid than polyethylene.

Polyurethane—Foam plastic, can be soft as for cushions, or hard as when used for insulation.

PVA—Polyvinyl acetate used as a glue or paint medium.

PVC—Polyvinyl chloride, a rigid thermoplastic.

Resin—Unpolymerized plastic.

Sink mark—A depression on the surface of a molded article opposite an interior rib where the plastic has shrunk.

Sprue—Mark left by nozzle on injection-molded plastic.

Terpolymer—A plastic made from three monomers.

Thermoforming—The shaping of heat-softened plastic.

Thermoplastic—A plastic that softens when heated.

Thermoset—A plastic that polymerizes under heat into a rigid final form.

Urea formaldehyde—A thermosetting amino plastic.

Vacuum forming—Means forcing a thermoplastic against a mold using atmospheric pressure.

Viscose rayon—Filaments of cellulose.

Vulcanization—The process of making rubber molding elastic.

Water white—A grade of color which looks like water.

Witness marks—Scars left by ejector pins when they push object out of a mold.

Glossary: Silver

Acanthus—Decorative leaf-shaped motif of classical origin, embossed, chased or applied.

Adam style—Neo-classical style c. 1765–1790, popularized by the brothers Adam.

Alloy—Composite of another metal, usually copper, with silver to produce more workable metal known as sterling silver.

Anneal—Practice of repeatedly heating silver to keep it malleable during working.

Annulet—Small ring-shaped decoration.

Anthemion—Decoration based on the honeysuckle flower.

Applied—Ornament or decoration added to integral shape.

Armorials—Coats of arms represented in full.

Assay—The testing of precious metals to ensure the correct proportion of base metal alloy. The assay office strikes relevant marks as proof of a successful test.

Associated—Combination of original and later pieces in a composite set; e.g. teapot and related stand.

Avoirdupois—British measurement, scale of weights.

Baluster—Pear shape found in candlesticks, wine glasses and cups from the end of the 16th century and especially during the early 18th century when it is found in coffee pots, tankards and jugs as well.

Bayonet fitting—Way of fitting covers to bases with small lugs twisted into slots.

Beading—Repetitive pattern, similar to a string of beads, commonly used as a border on edges and rims.

Bezel—Groove or flange around a rim.

Billet—Thumbpiece on a tankard or flagon.

Bleeding bowl—Shallow bowl with two ring handles, commonly mis-classified as a wine taster.

Boss—Rounded or raised (embossed).

Bound and reeded—A border pattern.

Bright cut—Faceted engraving used in late 18th, early 19th century.

Britannia metal—Pewter-like alloy without dangerous lead, introduced in the 1770s. Often as a base for 19th-century electroplated objects which were stamped E.P.B.M., "ElectroPlated Britannia Metal."

Britannia Standard—Higher standard for silver content in wrought plate which was the British standard supplanting sterling 1697–1720. Marked with lion's head in profile.

Bullet—Near spherical shape.

Bullion—Gold or silver before it is made up.

Calyx—Decoration like cupped leaves enfolding a bud.

Candelabra—Standing branched candlesticks.

Canteen—Matched set of boxed or cased flatware.

Cartouche—Decorative frame to a coat of arms.

Caryatid—Decorative motif of female figures.

Cast—Shaped by pouring molten material into a mold.

Caster—Container for condiments, sugar, spices with pierced cover for sprinkling.

Caudle cup—Two-handled drinking cup.

Chalice—Wine cup with a shallow bowl on a stem.

Charger—Large plate for serving meat.

Chased, chasing—Decoration on the surface of metal.

Chinoiserie—Chinese-style decorative motifs.

Chippendale—Mid 18th-century furniture designer Thomas Chippendale initiated several decorative motifs found in silver, especially a pie crust rim for salvers and waiters and "Chinese Chippendale" trellis-like borders on trays and coasters.

Close plating—Application of a layer of silver foil with a tin flux originally used to protect knife blades.

Comport—Fruit or dessert dish raised on a single foot.

Corded—Resembling twisted string.

C-scroll—Handle shape or decoration based on the letter "C".

Cut card work—Simple decoration based on leaf shapes cut out and usually soldered to the base of a bowl or cup.

Cymric—Derived from Celtic designs.

Diaper—Repetitive pattern of lozenges or diamonds.

Die-sinking—Manufacturing alternative to casting for feet, finials etc. Two halves of the part are hammered into dies, joined and filled with a lead/tin amalgam.

Die-stamping—Mechanical method to raise patterns with die and drop hammer.

Dished—Shaped with a slight concave curve.

Double-faced plate—Fused plate with silver on both sides.

Dredger—See "Caster".

Duty mark—Die with sovereign's head struck on all sizable silverware to show taxes had been paid.

Ecuelle—Shallow bowl with two flat handles and cover. Made in Quebec until early 18th century, rare.

Electroplate—The application of a thin layer of silver on base metal by electro-chemical means.

Electrotype—Fill a mold with silver by electro-chemical means.

Embossing—Way of raising a decoration on silver plate by working it from behind.

Epergne—Centerpiece "de resistance" popular in the 18th century often incorporating candlesticks and candy dishes.

Ewer—Large jug, accompanied by basin.

Extinguisher—Shaped like a dunce's cap on a stick, commonly found together with a chamberstick, for extinguishing candles.

Fancy back—Spoons with decoration at the back of the bowl.

Festoon—Drooping garland of flowers or fruit.

Filigree—Very fine silver wire openwork.

Finial—Topmost ornament on a piece, also end of cast spoons.

Flat chasing—Making the effect of an engraved pattern, not by cutting the metal away, but by impressing it.

Flatware—All tableware except knives.

Fly-punching—Piercing with mechanically-driven steel punches.

Foliate—Leaf-shaped decoration.

Fretwork—Pierced band or edge cut with a saw.

Gadroon—Repeating pattern of lobes.

Gauge—Thickness of metal.

Gold plating—Electrogilding technique for plating gold onto other metal.

Greek Key Pattern—Repetitive pattern of two interlaced ribbons or bands.

Hallmark—Mark struck by the assay office as proof that a gold or silver object is of stated purity.

Heraldry—The science of constructing coats of arms.

Holloware—Any article turned or cast in a hollow shape, including jugs, pots, tankards, etc.

Husk—Bell-shaped motif derived from corn husk.

Imperial measure—System of measuring volumes introduced in 1826.

Improved—Altered with decoration at a later date.

Incised—Marked by cutting into as opposed to applied or impressed.

Inverted baluster—Baluster upside down, like an inverted pear shape.

Judaica—Silver related to Jewish rites and rituals.

Lanceolate—Shaped like a lance blade or a stylized leaf shape.

Lap joint—A joint where two elements with "L" shaped cutouts are soldered.

Lattice—Crisscross pattern.

Loaded—Describing items filled with pitch to add weight and stability.

Lost wax—Ancient casting technique where a wax original is heated and melted out of a mold before silver or bronze is poured in.

Mantling—Plumes or feathers on either side of a coat of arms.

Marriage—Piece made up of fragments from two or more pieces.

Mask—Face of animal, bird or person used as decorative motif.

Mat—Non-shiny surface made with small punches.

Mazarine—Flat dish liner often decorated with piercing.

Milled edge—Shallowly serated like the edge of a coin.

Molding—Decorative rim or strip, applied or cast.

Mote spoon—Small spoon, decoratively pierced for skimming tea leaves, also has a sharp end for clearing clogged teaspouts.

Nef—Elaborate and bombastic salt cellar, nefs were revived during the romantic movement of the 19th century.

Nimbus—A halo.

Nozzle—The part of the candlestick into which the candle fits.

Palladian—Inspired by the designs of Antonio Palladio (1518–1580), who revived the taste for classical proportions and forms.

Parcel gilt—Contraction of "partially gilded."

Paten—Shallow dish to hold wafer at communion.

Pedestal foot—Similar to, but more substantial than, a stem support.

Peg tankard—A large drinking vessel of Scandinavian origin, resting on three or four cast feet with pegs marking off levels inside. Presumably so no individual could exceed his share during a communal drinking bout. Found in the North of England.

Pennyweight—Smallest measure of Troy weight, written: dwt.

Piecrust—Convex and concave curved border on a round object, popularized as part of a table design by Thomas Chippendale.

Pierced—Openwork done with chisels up to 1760, afterwards with a saw, and later by machine.

Pistol grip—Shape of a knife handle resembling the butt of an 18th-century pistol.

Planishing—A final step in making plate. A broad-faced hammer with a convex surface used to hammer out irregularities and smooth the surface.

Plinth—Square base at the bottom of a column.

Pricked—Engraving done with a needle point.

Provenance—Traceable ownership history of an antique or work of art.

Punched—Simple decorative motifs stamped on silver.

Quaich—Two-handled bowl, like a coverless écuelle, of Scottish origin.

Quatrefoil—Four-leaved or -lobed.

Raising stake—Cast iron anvil-like stake for shaping silver holloware.

Rat-tail—Tapering spine on back of a spoon bowl.

Regency—The period 1800–1830, in reference to the time (1811–1820) when George, Prince of Wales was Prince Regent.

Renaissance—The rebirth of classical arts in Italy from around 1400–1650.

Repoussé—Decorative technique combining embossing and chasing.

Rocaille—Seaside landscape with seaweed, shells, rocks, etc., on which French Rococo style was based.

Rococco—Asymmetric swirling design introduced in France c. 1730.

Sconce—Candle socket of candlestick, also candle holder with arms and a backplate for hanging on walls.

Sheffield plate—Same as fused plate.

Shoulder—Widest part of a stem or object.

Silver gilt—Silver that has been wholly or partially covered by gold.

Single-faced plate—Plated on one side only with silver.

Sinking block—Block of wood with a dish-shaped hollow for forming holloware.

Sovereign's head—Mark struck to show duty had been paid.

S Scroll—Handle based on the shape of the letter.

Stamping—Forming by hammering metal over a die bearing a reverse relief.

Sterling—Standard of purity for silver alloyed with copper since c. 1300. It guarantees 92.5 parts silver to 7.5 parts copper.

Strawberry dish—Shallow, fluted dessert dish.

Sucket fork—Two or three-pronged fork for spiking delicacies from their containers, sometimes with a spoon at the other end.

Swag—A heavier festoon.

Tastevin—A wine taster.

Tazza—Wide, shallow bowl on a single foot.

Tine—Prong of a fork.

Touch—Originally the test by touchstone to determine a metal's purity at an assay office. Later came to be associated with, and a synonym for, the marks struck by the office.

Trefoil—Having three leaves or lobes.

Troy weight—System for weighing and measuring precious metals and gems.

Tumbler cup—Round-bottomed drinking vessel.

Vinaigrette—Small box, usually silver for carrying something soaked in aromatic vinegar, used like a smelling bottle.

V joint—Joint made with a shaped notch and corresponding protrusion.

Waiter—Small silver salver.

Wine taster—Shallow bowl with one or two handles.

Glossary: Wood

Adze—An axe with the blade set at right angles to the handle. Used for rough shaping of timber.

Apron—Decorated front section between the front legs of a chair or chest.

Armoire—Large wardrobe, originally named for a piece that stored armour. Common in Quebec.

Ball and Claw—Foot shape, probably Chinese in origin, motif of a dragon's claw grasping a pearl. Popular in Queen Anne and Chippendale designs.

Bandage—Molding applied to legs in order to conceal repair, similar to collar.

Banding—Strip of wood laid into another wood of contrasting color.

Bergere—Low-backed chair of French design with arms running parallel to seat.

Birdcage—Mechanism under top of tilt-top table enabling it to be moved up and down.

Block Front—Door with solid wooden panels as opposed to glass or mirrors on cabinets and other case pieces.

Bombé—Literally "swelling" or bulging," refers to complex-curved shape of commodes.

Bonheur du Jour—Lady's small writing desk of French origin with pigeon holes at the back and drawers under the surface on slim tapered legs.

Bow front—Shape of front of commode or chest of drawers, swelling in the horizontal aspect only.

Bracket foot—Sawn-plank decoration covering feet of case pieces.

Breakfront—Describes piece of furniture with front jutting out past sides.

Butterfly hinge—Shape of iron hinge with flared sides, resembling butterfly wings.

Cabriole leg—"S" curved leg popular in 18th century furniture.

Carved up—When later carving has been added to plain surface of early piece.

Chaise longue—Simple, long couch-like chair.

Clout nail—Nail with square cut shaft and squarish head.

Cockbeading—Narrow molding projecting from edge of drawer fronts to protect the veneer.

Cockshead hinge—Like butterfly hinge, but "S" shaped.

Coffered panel—Panel that sits behind surrounding frame.

Collar—Additional molding to conceal repair work usually on table or chair legs.

Commode—Highly decorated chest of drawers originally French, often with bombé fronts.

Construction—Pertaining to framework as opposed to finish of a piece. Furniture construction comes in four types:

1. Board: flat planks nailed together.

2. Carcasse: Form constructed out of cheaper wood which is then veneered.

3. Frame: Skeletal frame into which panels are floated. Most French-Canadian furniture is of frame construction.

4. Joined: constructed of solid timber joined by doweled or mortise and tenon joins. Most English-Canadian furniture is joined.

Cornice—Molding that sits on top of and projects from top of bookcase, secretary or other cabinet.

Country furniture—Rural furniture made from local wood with function uppermost in the maker's mind. Also vernacular versions of fashionable styles.

Crest rail—Top rail of a chair, often decorated.

Cross rail—Horizontal rail running across chair back.

Dentil—regular crenellated border on French furniture, from the word for "tooth."

Distressed—Trade term for furniture that has been artificially aged by knocking or scratching the surface.

Dovetail—Way of joining boards at right angles, including:

Through dovetail: tail end of dovetail finished flush with outside surface.

Lapped dovetail: end finished flush with the surface of the piece into which it slots, suitable for veneering.

Mitred dovetail: fitted so the joint doesn't show.

Dowel—Wooden peg, precursor of nails.

Dowry Chest—Chest made for trousseau of young woman before marriage.

Drop leaf—Table with fixed central section and hinged, supported leaves.

Drop pull—Pear-shaped handle.

End grain—Grain exposed when wood is sawn perpendicular to the grain.

Escutcheon—Metal or bone plate surrounding keyhole.

Finial—Decorative knob.

Fluting—Grooves that run lengthwise down legs or columns.

Fretting—Pierced decoration cut with a fine-bladed fret saw.

Frieze—Border immediately below the cornice.

Gallery—Raised border of wood or metal that surrounds the edge of a table or desk top.

Gate leg—Stretchered leg attached to swivelling under-frame of a table.

Gesso—Plaster-like substance: a base for other finishes.

Girandole—Mirrored candle sconce.

Harlequin—Describes set of similar but not matched chairs.

"Improved"—Trade term for object that has been embellished with decoration to increase its value.

Knuckle—Projecting part of a wooden hinge.

Ladder back—Chair back formed of repeating horizontal elements.

Marquetry—Decorative surface made from small fitted pieces of veneer in a pattern.

Marriage—Object made up of two or more elements taken from different pieces. Particularly common among double-height furniture.

Mortise and tenon—Joining involving the fitting of a tongue (tenon) into a slot (mortise) secured by dowels.

Ogee—Slender "s" curve used on molding and bracket feet.

Ormolu—Gilded cast bronze.

Overhang—That part of a table top that projects beyond the main construction.

Overstuffed—A chair seat where the upholstery is attached to outside of seat frame.

Oyster veneer—Veneer cut from knotty sections of wood producing circular pattern resembling an oyster shell.

Pad foot—Often found at the end of a cabriole leg, a rounded foot resting on a pad.

Patina—Surface quality built up with years of polishing, handling, etc. Almost impossible to simulate and therefore important in assessing authenticity of a piece.

Plinth base—Lowermost portion of a piece that does not have feet.

Plinth molding—Built-up molding resembling classical plinth.

Prie-dieu—High-backed chair-like object with short legs. Used backwards to kneel on during prayer.

Provenance—Ownership history which can help establish authenticity.

Riven—Planks made by splitting rather than sawing.

Saddle seat—Carved seat especially in Windsor chairs that conform in shape to appropriate part of the body.

Semainier—French seven-drawered commode.

Shepherd's crook arm—Double curved arm rest and support.

Slatted—Flat parallel bars of a chair back.

Splat—Central upright of a chair back.

Stiles—Vertical parts of a furniture frame.

Strapwork—Relief carving taken from engravers' pattern books.

Stretcher—Horizontal supports between legs of chair or table.

Stringing—Thin strips of wood inlaid into decorative surface.

Tambour—Roll top or front desk.

Taper turned—Turned stretcher that tapers at ends.

Tenon—Tongue part of mortise and tenon joint.

Torchère—Single turned pillar fitted into a base and supporting a small circular, often dished, tray. Used for holding candles.

Underframe—Carcasse of tables and chairs.

Veneer—Finely figured wood cut very thin and glued to carcasse wood. Originally cut by a knife and quite thick. Today, it can be cut to a thickness of a fiftieth of an inch with special saws.

Whatnot—Small stand with graduated shelves for curios.

X-frame—Rudimentary support in an "x" shape for tables and chairs.

X Stretcher—Typically William and Mary design feature consisting of crossing stretchers often curved and sporting a decorative finial at the cross point.

Antiques and Flea Markets

Ontario

ABERFOYLE
The Aberfoyle Antique Market
(519) 763-1077
May–October Sundays
8:00 am to 5:00 pm
3 km N of 401

BARRIE
The 400 Market
(705) 436-1010
Dave Brown
All year–Saturday & Sunday
9:00 am to 5:00 pm
Hwy 400 8 km off Barrie 85A/B
400+ dealers
Special antique vendor section–
clothing, brass, jewelry, etc.

ELMVALE
The Elmvale Sales Barn &
Flea Market
(416) 278-4832
Mrs. Bates
April–November, Thursdays
11 am to 10 pm
2 km west of Elmvale, on Hwy 92
Started 30 years ago, 500+ dealers
Everything

FERGUS
Fergus Market
(519) 843-5221
All year—Saturday & Sunday
Sat 8:00 am to 5:00 pm
Sun 9:00 am to 5:00 pm
80 Vendors

GRAND BEND
The Pinery Antique Market
(519) 238-8382
April–October, Sunday
9:00 am to 5:00 pm
3 km S of Grand Bend on Hwy 21
200 Vendors

HAMILTON
Circle M Antique & Flea Market
(416) 642-4925
Helen Dimillo
All Year, Sunday
10:00 am to 5:00 pm
4 km W of Hwy 6 on Hwy 5
Clappison's Corners
Started 20 years ago, 150 Vendors
Antiques (tools, toys, furniture,
coins, etc).

Steel City Flea Market
(416) 545-4747
All Year, Sundays
10:00 am to 5:00 pm
29 Linden St.

JORDAN
Jordan Valley Flea Market
(416) 562-5936
May–October, Sunday
9:00 am to 5:00 pm
2964 Regional Rd.
125 Vendors

KINGSTON
The Odessa Antique Show
(613) 283-1168
Bill Dobson
August 8 & 9
Saturday 2:00 to 9:00 pm, early
admission $20
Sunday 7:00 am to 4:00 pm, $4.00
The Odessa Fairgrounds, (Wilton Rd.
exit off 401 at Odessa)
150 Vendors
A complete range of antiques &
collectibles. No-reproduction policy
in effect.

The Kingston Winter Antique Show
(613) 283-1168
Bill Dobson
February 6 & 7, 1993
Saturday & Sunday 10:00 am to
5:00 pm
The Kingston Portsmouth Olympic
Harbour Centre
50 invited dealers exhibiting a
diverse selection of quality antiques.

LONDON
Forest City Flea Market
(519) 439-7767
Bill Marshal
All year, Sundays
10:30 am to 4:30 pm
Western Fairgrounds London
150–250 Vendors

MORRISBURG
McHaffie's Flea Market
(613) 543-9000
Sheila McHaffie
All Year, Sundays
9:00 am to 5:00 pm
3 Km N on Hwy 31
Started in May 1980, 160 Vendors
Collectibles, new & used, crafts,
antiques, furniture, glassware, etc.

NIAGARA FALLS
Chippawa Flea Market
(416) 295-4815
All Year, Sundays
9:00 am to 5:00 pm
8249 Dock St.
100 Vendors

Niagara Falls Flea Market
(416) 356-8101
All Year, Sundays
9:00 am to 5:00 pm
4735 Drummond Rd.
100–130 Vendors

OSHAWA
Oshawa Flea Market
(416) 683-5290
Ken MacKenzie
All Year, Sundays
9:00 am to 4:30 pm
727 Wilson Rd. S. of Hwy 401
Started in 1980, 80 Vendors
Electronics, jewelry, used &
collectibles, crafts, used records, etc.

PETERBOROUGH
The Barn
(705) 741-2560
All Year, Saturdays & Sundays
9:00 am to 5:00 pm
Fowlers Corners on 7B

Peterborough Flea Market
(705) 749-0611
All Year, Saturdays & Sundays
9:00 am to 5:00 pm
Morrow Park Bldg., Landsdowne E.
80–150 Vendors

PICKERING
Pickering Flea Market
(416) 427-0754 Alison Vieira
(416) 683-2620 George Nunes
All Year–Sundays
7:00 am to 5:00 pm
1899 Brock Rd. Metro East Centre
Started in December 1973,
800 Vendors
Antiques, furniture, electronics,
clothing (mostly new products)

PORT DALHOUSIE
Factory Outlet Flea Market CWB
(416) 684-3066
Larry Sullivan
All Year, Sundays
9:00 am to 5:00 pm
46 Turner Cres. off Lincoln Ave.
Started in 1989, 260 Vendors
New, used, collectibles, antiques,
furniture, glassware, jewelry, etc.

ST. CATHARINES
The Family Flea Market Club
(416) 682-4660
All Year, Sundays
9:00 am to 4:30 pm
55 Oakdale Ave.
200 Vendors

ST. GEORGE
St. George Flea Market
(519) 448-1831
Stella Fox
May–August, Sundays
10:00 am to 4:00 pm
South Dunfries Community Centre
Started 6 years ago, 80 Vendors
Antiques, sports cards, crafts, home
baked goods, glassware, etc.

STITTSVILLE
Stittsville Flea Market
(613) 836-5612
Hal Raycroft
All Year, Sundays
9:00 am to 5:00 pm
6174 Hazeldean Rd.
Started in 1971, 250 Vendors
Antiques, collectibles, furniture,
clothing, period furniture, jewelry,
hockey card vendors, etc.

STOUFFVILLE
Stouffville Stockyards, Home of the
Big Flea Market
(416) 640-3813
Rob Shannon
All Year, Saturdays & Sundays
Sat 8:00 am to 4:00 pm
Sun 9:00 am to 4:00 pm
Hwy 47, outskirts of Stouffville
Started 35 years ago, 300–600
vendors
Summer: antiques, outside vegetable
markets, regular products, etc.

TORONTO
The Harbourfront Antique Market
(416) 340-8377
All Year,
Tues–Thur 11:00 am to 6:00 pm
Sat 10:00 am to 5:00 pm
Sun 8:00 am to 6:00 pm
390 Queens Quay West, Toronto
100–200 Vendors

Antiques Fairs
Ontario
ABERFOYLE
Flamboro Antique Show
(416) 685-1225
July & August
Early Bird Admission: $25
Hwy 401, Exit 299, Aberfoyle

ANCASTER
Ancaster Heritage Doll Show & Sale
(416) 389-9169
October
Admission: $2
Marritt Hall, Ancaster Fairgrounds,
Hwy 53

BALA
Muskoka Nostalgia & Collectibles
Show
(705) 762-5631
July
10:00 am to 5:00 pm
Maple Street, Bala

BURLINGTON
20th Burlington Antique Show
(416) 335-2686
October
680 Plains Rd West, Burlington

CAMBRIDGE
Cambridge (GALT) Antique
Show & Sale
(519) 442-6297
Bill Gerbrandt
October
Duncan McIntosh Centre-Hall,
Cambridge (GALT)

ELORA
Antiques in Elora
(519) 442-6297
Bill Gerbrandt
July
Elora Community Centre

FLESHERTON
Antiques at Flesherton
(519) 442-6297
Bill Gerbrandt
October
Flesherton Arena

LONDON
Can. Am. Antique Show & Sale
(519) 686-7992
P.R.Promotions
June & September
Fanshawe Conservation Area,
Clarke Road

MAXVILLE
The Glengarry Gathering Antique
Heritage Show
(613) 528-4453 ; 678-2873
September
Maxville Fairgrounds

MILTON
Flamboro Antique Show
(416) 685-1225
June
Conservation Area, Milton

ODESSA
Odessa Antique Show & Sale
(613) 283-1168
August
Odessa Fairgrounds, 10 Miles West
of Kingston on Hwy 2, just South of
Hwy 401, Exit 599 (Wilton Road)

TORONTO
Antique Show & Sale
(416) 483-6471
Heritage Antique Show & Sales
September
O'Keefe Centre, 1 Front St. East

Heritage Antique Market
(416) 483-6471
September
Heritage Antique Show & Sale
Bayview Village Shopping Centre
Bayview Ave. & Sheppard Ave.

WOODSTOCK
Nostalgia-Rama '91
(416) 278-7363
Bill Lavall
September
Auditorium, Fairgrounds,
Woodstock

Quebec

KNOWLTON
Knowlton 92 Antique Show & Sale
(514) 933-7731

MONTREAL
Antiques Bonaventure
(514) 933-6375

Cavendish Fall Winter Show
(514) 933-6375

The Delta Montreal Monthly Sunday
Antique Fairs
(514) 489-1735
Lana Harper
Sunday 10:30 am to 5:00 pm
475 President Kennedy, Montreal
15–20 Vendors
Antique English porcelain and
engravings; silver; jewelry;
Canadiana; books; continental glass
& porcelain; orientalia; collectibles
etc.

The Quebec Antiques Fair
(613) 283-1168;
Bill Dobson
July 4 & 5
Saturday 2:00 pm to 9:00 pm (early
admission $20)
Sunday 7:00 am to 4:00 pm ($4)
Seaway Park, St. Lambert (between
Champlain bridge & Jacques Cartier
bridge)
150 vendors
Complete range of antiques &
collectibles with no-reproduction
policy in effect.

ROCKBURN
Chateauguay Valley Antique
Association Exhibition
(514) 264-5615
Judy Maither
August 22 & 23
Saturday & Sunday 8:00 am to 5:00
pm
1743 First Concession, Rockburn
30–35 Vendors
Arts, crafts & antiques.

NORTH HATLEY
Antique & Folk Art Show
(819) 842-4380

Manitoba

WINNIPEG
Winnipeg Doll Show & Sale
(204) 694-0667
Irene Henderson
October 18, 1992
Sunday 10:00 am to 4:00 pm
The International Inn,
Wellington & Berry
50 Vendors
Dolls, toys & doll related items.

Saskatchewan

REGINA
Antiques & Collectibles Sale
(306) 522-7580
Noreeta Finn
April 25 & 26, 1992
Saturday 10:00 am to 6:00 pm
Sunday 10:00 am to 5:00 pm
200 Lakeshore Drive
60–65 Vendors
Antiques & collectibles.

B.C.

BURNABY
Tosland Antique & Collectible Show
(604) 431-0900
Bob Knapton
March 19, 20 & 21, 1992
June 11, 12 & 13, 1992
November 19, 20 & 21, 1992
Thursday, 5:00 pm to 10:00 pm
Friday 10:00 am to 10:00 pm
Saturday 10:00 am to 5:00 pm
7325 McPherson Ave, Burnaby
95 Vendors
All antiques & collectibles.

KELOWNA
The Okanagan Doll & Toy Show
(604) 764-2675; 769-4365
Mary Miller/Ruth Jacobsen
September 27, 1992
Sunday 10:00 am to 4:00 pm
The Lions Community Centre,
West Bank
50 Vendors
Antique dolls & toys.

Nova Scotia

HALIFAX
Great Atlantic Collectors Experience
(902) 369-2289

A national listing of flea markets and antique shows in books of this length must necessarily be incomplete. Our apologies are extended to any market or show that has been inadvertently omitted.

Rebate for Visitors: GST (Goods & Service Tax)

GST and Visitors to Canada

Under the Goods and Services Tax (GST), most goods and services sold or provided in Canada are taxed at the rate of seven per cent.

A pamphlet available from Revenue Canada explains how visitors to Canada can claim a rebate of the GST they pay on short-term accommodation (hotel, motel or similar lodging) and on most consumer goods they purchase to take home.

The rebate application included in the pamphlet is divided into Sections A, B, C, D, E and F. Claimants must fill out each section. Please remove the application and follow the detailed instructions on the reverse. Additional information is provided in the pamphlet for completing Sections D, E and F.

To obtain a copy of the pamphlet, further information or assistance, please write to:

Revenue Canada, Customs and Excise
Visitors Rebate Program
Ottawa, Canada K1A 1J5

or call, toll-free from anywhere in Canada, 1-800-66VISIT. If you are outside Canada, please call (613) 991-3346.

Basic Information

You can apply for a GST rebate if:
• you are not a resident of Canada; and
• your total claim is for at least $7 of GST (that is, the amount you paid for purchases of goods and/or short-term accommodation in Canada is $100 [Canadian] or more).

Goods qualify for a rebate if:
• GST was paid on the goods
• they were purchased for use outside Canada; and
• they were removed from Canada within 60 days of purchase.

If the seller ships your purchase outside Canada directly, you will not have to pay the GST at the time of purchase, therefore you will not be able to claim a rebate.

You can also claim a rebate for the GST you paid in Canada on short-term accommodations, such as hotel and motel rooms. However, if you purchase the accommodation outside of Canada (for example, as part of a package), you will not be able to claim a rebate.

There is NO rebate for the GST paid on:

- services such as dry cleaning and shoe repair;
- goods left in Canada;
- meals and restaurant charges;
- camping and trailer-park fees;
- wine, liquor, beer or other alcoholic beverages;
- tobacco products;
- automotive fuels;
- basic groceries, agricultural and fish products, prescription drugs and medical devices (no GST is paid on these goods).

How to Claim a Rebate

You can claim your rebate by mailing the completed rebate application form to:

Revenue Canada, Customs and Excise
Visitor's Rebate Program
Ottawa, Canada K1A 1J5

You must include the original bill of sale with your application. Photocopies of receipts will not be accepted. Accommodation receipts must show evidence of the number of nights of accommodation supplied.

For purchases that must be registered in your own country, such as cars, you must include the original bill of sale together with a copy of the registration outside Canada.

Your original receipts together with supporting documents will be returned to you separately from your rebate cheque in case you want to apply for a refund of the provincial tax you may have paid in certain provinces. Provincial Tourist Information Centres can help you with these refund programs.

NOTE: The receipts you submit with your application for a provincial tax refund will not be returned to you. Therefore, we suggest that you claim your federal GST rebate first. Your original receipts will be returned to you so that you can claim a provincial sales tax refund.

Claim Period

You have one year from the date you purchased the goods and/or accommodation to claim your GST rebate. If you mail your rebate application form, you can only apply once every three months.

Visitors to Canada who make occasional purchases of goods for their businesses can file one GST rebate application per month. Otherwise they must use the General Rebate Application form to claim a GST rebate on business purchases exported from Canada. To obtain a copy of the general form, call one of these telephone numbers:

Toll-Free inside Canada
1-800-66VISIT

Outside Canada
(613) 991-3346

Acknowledgements

Thanks to the following people who gave of their time and expertise during the research of this book:

Julia Fenn, ROM; Patricia Proctor, ROM; Bill Dobson, The Upper Canadian; Gary Borton, Popular Culture; Ross Young, 20th Century; Hollis Frampton, Another Man's Poison; Don Lake, D&E Lake; Marlene Wilson; Marlene Cook; Susan Wilson, Craig Black and to Gulshan Sippy who provides invaluable support.

Bibliography

Collard, Elizabeth, *Nineteenth-Century Pottery and Porcelain in Canada*, Kingston & Montreal, McGill-Queen's University Press, 1984.

Cross, W.K., publisher; *The Charlton 1991 Collector's Guide to Ontario*; Toronto & Birmingham MI, The Charlton Press, 1991.

Dorn, Sylvia O'Neill, *The Insider's Guide to Antiques, Art and Collectibles*, New York, Doubleday & Co. Inc., 1974.

Feild, Rachel, *Macdonald Guide to Buying Antique Furniture*, London, Macdonald & Co. (publishers) Ltd., 1984.

Feild, Rachel, *Macdonald Guide to Buying Antique Silver & Sheffield Plate*, London & Sydney, Macdonald & Co. (publishers) Ltd., 1988.

Fennimore, Donald L., *The Knopf Collector's Guide to American Antiques;* Silver & Pewter, New York, Alfred A. Knopf, Inc., 1984.

Forty, Adrian, *Objects Of Desire; Design & Society from Wedgwood to IBM*, New York, Pantheon Books, 1986.

Frankel, Betsey, ed., *The Encyclopedia of Collectibles*, New York, Time/Life Books, 1978.

Guillet, Edwin C., *Pioneer Days in Upper Canada*, Toronto, University of Toronto Press, 1963.

Jones, Mark ed., *Fake? The Art of Deception*, Berkeley, University of California Press, 1990.

Katz, Sylvia, *Plastics: Common Objects, Classic Designs*, New York, Harry N. Abrams, Inc., 1984.

Kovel, Ralph & Terry, *Kovel's Antiques & Collectibles Fix-It Source Book*, New York, Crown Publishers, Inc., 1990.

Kovel, Ralph & Terry, *Kovel's Guide to Selling Your Antiques & Collectibles*, New York, Crown Publishers, Inc., 1987.

McIntyre, John, "Collecting Canadian Furniture" *The Canadian Collector*, July/Aug. '81, pp 28–31.

McLaren, George, *Nova Scotia Glass*, Halifax, Nova Scotia Museum, 1971.

Ohrbach, Barbara Milo, *Antiques At Home*, New York, Clarkson N. Potter, Inc., 1989.

Osborne, Harold, ed., *The Oxford Companion to the Decorative Arts*, London, The Oxford University Press, 1975.

Pain, Howard, *The Heritage of Upper Canadian Furniture*, Toronto, Key Porter Books, 1984.

Palardy, Jean, *The Early Furniture of French Canada*, Toronto, MacMillan, 1963.

Smith, Jean & Elizabeth, *Collecting Canada's Past*, Scarborough, Prentice Hall, 1974.

Sommer, Elyse, *Textile Collector's Guide*, Sovereign Books, 1978.

Spence, Hilda & Kevin, *A Guide to Early Canadian Glass*, Don Mills, Longmans Canada, 1966.

Spendlove, F. St. George, *The Face of Early Canada*, Toronto, The Ryerson Press, 1958.

Stevens, Gerald, *Canadian Glass, 1825–1925*, Toronto, The Ryerson Press, 1967.

Stevens, Gerald, *In A Canadian Attic*, Toronto, The Ryerson Press, 1962.

Webster, Donald Blake, "Furniture Sleuthing" *The Canadian Collector*, Mar/Apr '76, pp 16–18.

Webster, Donald Blake, ed. *The Book of Canadian Antiques*, Toronto, McGraw-Hill Ryerson Ltd, 1974.

Webster, Donald Blake, "The Identification of English Canadian Furniture, 1780–1840" *Antiques*, Jan. '76, pp 164–179.